EXERCISES
AND TESTS
FOR
JOURNALISTS

EXERCISES AND TESTS FOR JOURNALISTS

BASED ON THE REVISED EDITION OF
GRAMMAR FOR JOURNALISTS

E. L. CALLIHAN
HAROLD L. NELSON
WAYNE A. DANIELSON

CHILTON BOOK COMPANY
Philadelphia   New York   London

Published in Philadelphia by Chilton Book Company
and simultaneously in Ontario, Canada,
by Thomas Nelson & Sons, Ltd.

ISBN 0-8019-5560-2
Library of Congress Catalog Card Number 75-127597
Designed by Harry Eaby
Manufactured in the United States of America by
Graphic Arts Composition, Inc. and Vail-Ballou Press, Inc.

Preface

Exercises were included in the first edition of *Grammar for Journalists*, published by the Ronald Press in 1957. In the completely revised edition, published by the Chilton Book Company in the fall of 1969, the exercises were deliberately omitted. The book was streamlined, with only introductory quizzes used at the beginning of each chapter, in order to make it valuable as a reference aid for practicing journalists as well as a textbook for journalism students.

Dr. Harold L. Nelson, Dean of the School of Journalism at the University of Wisconsin, and Dr. Wayne A. Danielson, Dean of the School of Communication at the University of Texas, have composed and updated the Nelson-Danielson Tests, which were based on the first edition of *Grammar for Journalists* and which have been administered in eighteen schools and departments of journalism.

The exercises should provide ample drill material for students who find themselves deficient in any area of grammar, spelling or punctuation. Although only one exercise has been written for each of eight chapters in *Grammar for Journalists*, that should be sufficient for the student's practice needs. Two or three exercises for each of eight other chapters should provide the maximum amount of drill material needed, and should afford both student and teacher a choice of the most needed material. For the chapter on spelling, thirteen exercises have been provided. Most of the exercises come directly from the media—newspapers, magazines and radio-television broadcasts. In many instances, errors have been added to make the exercises more comprehensive.

The student should not be dismayed if he finds himself deficient in many areas of grammar, spelling and punctuation. Most students have such shortcomings simply because the fundamentals of grammar and composition are no longer adequately emphasized in high school and in the first year of college English. As pointed out in Chapter One of *Grammar for Journalists*, 100 American editors, when asked what they regard as the greatest weaknesses of men and women entering journalism today, succinctly replied: "Grammar, spelling and punctuation."

The student must therefore master the fundamentals. By all means, he must be sure to drill, drill, drill! He cannot learn grammar merely by reading about the principles and the rules; he must analyze and practice writing. The exercises in this workbook are designed to provide the student with the kind of practice he needs most.

The study of English—a living, growing language— should be a lifetime effort of every journalist. The journalist puts what he has learned—or not learned—into print or on the air almost every day of his life.

Teachers will find they can make use of the exercises in many ways. In using the first edition of *Grammar for Journalists*, in which the exercises followed each chapter, instructors of news writing and reporting classes in many schools have found it worthwhile to require all students to do most of the exercises. In other schools, instructors have found it necessary to require students deficient in certain areas of grammar to do only the exercises that deal with their deficiencies.

Journalism teachers will find that they can continue to use the exercises, as well as the textbook, in advanced classes. Instructors using the first edition of *Grammar for Journalists* in editing classes have found it highly profitable to require editing students to study the exercises pertinent to their particular deficiencies.

In many schools, it has also been found most beneficial to require students of feature writing, magazine article writing, or any advanced writing to study the exercises in Part II of *Grammar for Journalists*. Before doing the exercises, the student should read Part II, which covers unity, emphasis, coherence or clarity, and variety of expression. No journalism teacher needs to be told that the journalist's use of words, figures of speech, sentences and paragraphs determines his writing style — and that writing style identifies a writer either as a master craftsman or as just an ordinary journalist. Study and drill in unity, emphasis, coherence and variety of expression cannot be stressed too much.

Finally, for improving students' punctuation and spelling, the teacher should find abundant material here to serve the needs of students who require additional study and drill. Many undergraduate, and even graduate, students are careless spellers.

I hope that students and teachers of journalism find in the revised exercises exactly what they need in the way of drill material to meet their respective goals of becoming and preparing expert journalists. A teacher's manual of corrected exercises is being published simultaneously.

E. L. CALLIHAN
Dallas, Texas
July, 1969

2
The Journalist's Chief Tool— The Sentence

EXERCISES

I. Follow these four steps in doing the first exercise: (1) draw one line under each simple (essential) subject in each clause of the sentence; (2) draw two lines under each simple (essential) predicate in each clause of the sentence; (3) in sentences having more than one clause, identify each clause as independent or dependent by writing the abbreviation *(Ind.)* or *(Dep.)* directly above it; (4) at the end of each sentence, classify the sentence's use and form.

EXAMPLES:

                    (Ind.)   (Dep.)
Johnston, not his subordinates, was the one who gave the order. (Declarative, Complex)
                (Dep.)   (Ind.)
    If Leonard does not choose to run, whom will the Democrats choose as a candidate? (Interrogative, Complex)

The <u>note</u> demanding the freedom of the 82 Pueblo crew-
        (Ind.)
men <u>was</u> <u>delivered</u> to North Korea by the State Department
spokesman, Robert J. McCloskey. (Declarative, Simple)
        (Ind.)
<u>Students</u> <u>jeered</u> and <u>wept</u> and <u>hurled</u> cobblestones, but
        (Ind.)
into Prague <u>came</u> <u>hundreds</u> of Soviet T-54 tanks, to take
over. (Declarative, Compound) (In the first independent
clause, there is a triple predicate. In the second clause, the
subject comes after the predicate, in inverted order.)
        (Dep.)
When <u>triumph</u> <u>was</u> certain, <u>Senator Kennedy</u> and <u>those</u>
(Ind.)
closest to him <u>went</u> down in two elevators to the Embassy
        (Ind.)
Room and <u>he</u> <u>made</u> a victory speech. (Declarative, Compound-Complex) (Note that the first independent clause
has a compound subject.)

1. James Earl Ray's colorless and hangdog presence had
led some to give credence to a theory that King's killing was
a conspiracy and that Ray's part in it was, at most, that of a
hapless decoy.

2. Thomas Everett Dickerson, along with his younger
brother, was arrested for auto theft.

3. Dickerson, who boasts of his prowess with a gun,
takes his place on the FBI "ten most wanted" list.

4. Before his captors completed the routine check which revealed him as a nationally sought fugitive, Dickerson escaped.

5. He sawed the bars of a cell in the county jail at Sandy Hook, Ky., and squeezed through a hole 14 inches wide and eight inches high.

6. "(You) Come out of there quick, or I will fire!"

7. "He reached toward his back, and I fired one shot."

8. On the floor near Landon was a long-bladed knife.

9. The "Julia" show, which made its debut in 1968, soon leaped into the top ten television shows, and it was earning the highest audience ratings before the end of the year.

10. How did Dustin soar to stardom in just one picture?

II. This exercise contains all the types of errors discussed in chapter two. Correct the errors by typing or rewriting the sentences, or by copy editing if you know how to use copy editing symbols.

1. Mayor Johnson doubts that the city's budget can be

balanced this year, in fact, he is doubtful that it can be balanced within two years.

2. Miss Kirzenstein chopped two-tenths of a second off her own world record. While Barbara Ferrell of Los Angeles, who had set an Olympic record of 22.8 in the semifinals, finished fourth in 22.9.

3. They can depend on McCool, he is a faithful party man.

4. Spindly Bob Beamon is an outstanding long jumper. One of the best in the world.

5. A chain of Myers department stores are to be set up in the Southwest.

6. "Actually, we don't know which team is No. 1, so your guess is as good as any right now," said Coach Hayes.

7. Behind him were two Buckeyes breathing down his neck, before him, coming in fast, was the Ohio State safety man.

8. The mayor, as well as five councilmen, are expected to vote for the resolution.

9. The new drug, he pointed out, has been used with amazing results but it must be used, he added, only in advanced stages of the disease.

10. Hard-running fullback Jim Otis and Rex Kern marched the Buckeyes 69 yards, then Otis scored from the one.

11. Housley's knee has failed to heal completely, therefore he may see little action against Baylor Saturday.

12. In one scene of an anti-colonialist play, a group of blacks are shown portraying African whites praying for a dead soldier.

3
Know the Parts
of Speech

EXERCISES

In the following news story, which was headlined "Nixon 'Socks it to 'Em,'" identify which part of speech each word is by writing above it the appropriate abbreviation: *V.* for verb; *N.* for noun; *Pr.* for pronoun; *Adj.* for adjective; *Adv.* for adverb; *Prep.* for preposition; *Con.* for conjunction; or *Int.* for interjection. If the words of a verb phrase are separated, write *V.* above each part. A good mental exercise is to classify each noun, pronoun, adjective, and adverb as you come to it, but you need to write only the abbreviation that tells which part of speech the word is. In identifying conjunctions, don't overlook connective adverbs and conjunctive adverbs.

Richard Nixon, the former Republican "straight man,"

is showing that little bit of rebel that has always been irre-

sistible to the young.

And this may prove the most important acquisition in the New Nixon personality.

In short, Nixon is speaking the language of the young voter. The result is more exposure of Nixon the Man and less of Nixon the calculating, impersonal politician whose rigidness and washed-out television look contributed to his defeat in 1960.

In Nixon's appearance Friday at Moody Coliseum, there was more talk of football than politics, more talk of life than doom, more talk of vitality than senility.

And there was the now inevitable, "Sock it to 'em," which brings down the rafters. . . .

However, Nixon is doing the selling. And apparently the young public is in the buying mood.

"Oh, I would love to hug him!" exclaimed one pert 16-year-old blonde.

"That is something I never heard anyone say about Nixon in 1960," commented one newsman.

4

The Framework
of the Sentence

EXERCISES

I. In the following sentences, select the correct word from the parentheses. Then underline the essential parts of each sentence: simple subject, simple predicate, direct object. If a verb does not have a direct object, tell whether it is intransitive or linking by writing *Intr.* or *Link.* above it.

1. The crippled child had been (lying, laying) on the beach all night.

2. (Set, Sit) up, Rover!

3. The water from White Rock Lake tastes (badly, bad) this week.

4. Complaining that he felt (bad, badly), he (lay, laid) down under a tree.

5. If the new vases arrive (safe, safely), (set, sit) them on the mantle.

II. In the sentences in this exercise, underline each simple verb and verb phrase you find and write the appropriate abbreviation above it: *Tr., Intr.* or *Link.* There is one transitive passive verb; mark it *Tr. Pass.* Remember that some sentences have two or more clauses and that each clause has a verb or verb phrase.

Tr.

EXAMPLES: The men <u>had bagged</u> three ducks.

Intr.

One hunter <u>fell</u> into the lake.

Link.

He <u>looked</u> silly.

Link.

The mother <u>was</u> happy.

1. The plane must have been flying too low.

2. Meredith could barely lift his throwing arm.

3. Suddenly the fabulous Leroy Keyes burst into the open and scored on a 16-yard dart.

4. Lying in the gutter was an unconscious man.

5. Who will be Syracuse's next mayor?

6. All the civilians killed were dependents of military personnel, including eight children and two women.

7. The arrested youth declared defiantly, "I will not go back to that town."

8. The crippled plane crashed in flames into an Air Force housing project Thursday, killing 16 persons, six of them children. Eight of the plane crew were killed.

III. In the following sentences, identify the usages of the italicized words and phrases. Write the appropriate abbreviation above each: *Subj.* for subject; *Obj.* for object of the verb; *Pred. N.* for predicate noun; *Pred. Pron.* for predicate pronoun; *Pred. Adj.* for predicate adjective. In some sentences, you must choose between words which are in the nominative or the objective case.

1. *(Who, Whom)* will be the next *chairman?*

2. *(Who, Whom)* will *they* select for chairman?

3. *It* is *(him, he) (who, whom)* must be considered for the chairmanship.

4. *To win* a majority in Congress is the Republicans' first *objective.*

5. The Republicans' first *objective* is *to win* a majority in Congress.

6. *He* quit the *stage*, became a Knoxville *businessman* and achieved moderate *success*.

5
More About Verbs

EXERCISES

I. In this exercise, do three things: (1) cross out the *incorrect* form of the verb within the parentheses; (2) show why you chose each form by writing *Intr.* above each intransitive verb and *Tr.* above each transitive verb; (3) underline the object of each transitive verb. There is one transitive passive verb; mark it Tr. Pass.

1. Headline: What (Lays, Lies) in Future for Alaska?

2. TV broadcast: One out of ten (lies, lays) dead on the beach.

3. Pugh (lay, laid) flat on his back on the Cotton Bowl turf. Early in the first half he had been (lain, laid) on a stretcher, his left knee a mass of torn ligaments.

4. "(Lay, Lie) down and be quiet for an hour," he ordered.

5. The girl had carefully (lain, laid) her clothes on the bed.

6. In a world where man had so much control of human destiny, what values would (underlie, underlay) key decisions?

7. The Colt tackles were really (laying, lying) for Anderson on the play.

8. The six-year-old boy was just (setting, sitting) there in the ruins, trying hard not to cry.

9. (Set, Sit) it down over there.

10. The Ohio State football team (sat, set) back and enjoyed the movie of their game with Michigan.

11. "(Sit, Set) there by the fire until your clothes dry out," the lieutenant told him.

12. The boy (shone, shined) the old farmer's shoes until they (shone, shined) like new.

II. In this exercise, cross out the *incorrect* form of the verb within the parentheses. Above each form that you choose as correct, write the abbreviation for its tense: *Pr.* for present, *Pt.* for past, *Fut.* for future, *Cond.* for conditional, *Pr. Perf.* for present perfect, *Pt. Perf.* for past perfect, *Pt. Part.* for past participle, or *Fut. Perf.* for future perfect.

1. A burglary ring of Dallas youngsters (lead, led) by a nine-year-old boy faced juvenile delinquency charges Wednesday.

2. Yesterday Patrick Welch (led, lead) the St. Patrick's Day procession down Main Street.

3. She could have (sung, sang) "Yes, We Have No Bananas" and (drawn, drew) an ovation.

4. This was the year of the runner, and numerous players like O. J. Simpson of Southern Cal, Jim Otis of Ohio State and Ron Johnson of Michigan (shined, shone) brightest, to make the 1968 season one of expanded scoring.

5. Suddenly the children (sprang, sprung) from their hiding place and (sung, sang) "Happy Birthday to You."

6. He charged that the commissioners had not (payed, paid) him the stipulated fee.

7. After questioning the youth for nine hours, the detectives (rang, rung, wrang, wrung) a confession from him.

8. H. L. Hunt (strove, strived) hard to accumulate his first million.

9. He said that he could (loose, lose) his fortune, but he had (chose, chosen, choosen) to gamble everything on drilling for oil in that area.

10. The ground was (froze, frozen) over, and one pipe had (burst, bursted, busted).

11. He dived in and (drug, dragged) the body of the (drowned, drown) girl from the creek.

12. The cowboy's body (hanged, hung) there for almost an hour before it was removed. Later it was (proved, proven) that he had not been guilty.

13. The Jordans (use, used) to live in San Jose.

14. Joe Namath has (proven, proved) that he is one of the greatest passers in professional football.

15. Mrs. Farmer had (sewn, sewed, sowed, sown) on a dress all day, and Mr. Farmer had (sewn, sewed, sowed, sown) about 25 acres of wheat.

III. Rewrite or type the sentences, making the necessary corrections. Underline each correction you make, and write above it the letter which indicates the type of error you have corrected: A. incorrect form of verb, B. unnecessary shift in tense, C. wrong voice, D. wrong mood, E. wrong person of verb.

1. Lisa Hall stepped onto the Cabaña Bon Vivant stage last night and sung with a stage presence so satisfying that one didn't ask for anything else. The pretty, friendly blonde has sung as a former Lilt girl for CBS.

2. He warned that some government operations must cease unless quick remedial action were taken.

3. Jim Henry of Indiana dove to an AAU diving championship with 484.05 points.

4. The hard tackling by the Georgia Bulldogs had really began to tell.

5. Crafty Dancer has started 15 times, won seven, ran second three times and third once.

6. Had the tight end simply fell and concentrated on the ball, he would have caught it.

7. The ball should be grasped firmly; then you release it with a quick twist of the wrist.

8. The candidate for Place Four seemed to have his two opponents soundly beat.

9. The outstanding player had proved to be Chris Gilbert, who had ran for the third greatest number of yards in Southwest Conference history.

10. Spillane led you to believe that the butler is the murderer, and you do not discover that Julie is the guilty one until the final paragraph.

6
Properties of Nouns and Pronouns

EXERCISES

I.A. Write the singular possessive of each of these:

1. the boy......coat

2. Gray and Perry......shop

3. John Keats......poems

4. Mr. Holmes......mansion

5. his wife......property

6. the puppy......ball

7. a hero......welcome

8. the princess......escort

9. a witch......broomstick

10. the notary public......sign

I.B. Write the plural possessive of each of these:

1. witch......broomsticks

2. child......toys

3. Holmes......autos

4. mouse......tails

5. alumnus......reunion

6. wife......shares

7. farmer......magazines

8. hobo......shoes

9. fox......tails

10. woman......dresses

11. the Charles......reigns

12. policeman......beats

II. Rewrite the following sentences, correcting the errors or improving the expressions.

1. The Clinton Dad's Club will hold it's first Dads and Sons banquet Tuesday night.

2. "I dont mind you making a few popsicles in the freezer," the mother told her daughter.

3. The union gave 48 hours notice before striking, and the strike was settled in one hours time.

4. Leslie did not bother with the smallest deers antlers, but he had the two largest deers antlers mounted.

5. This coat is your's, but Harrys is not here.

6. The two Harry's suits look alike.

7. Ellis met Quarrys' second-round rush with a sustained attack. Ellis's hard right to the stomach made the challengers knees buckle.

8. The Volunteers new coach would make no comment concerning his teams' prospects.

9. Although he said he could do a good days work, he was unable in three days time to show he could do the work satisfactorily.

10. This one is our's, but who's is that?

11. Prospects of them being written into labor law were considered gloomy today.

12. Give him two tablespoonsful every four hours'.

13. The men servant's quarters were searched.

14. She could not bear the thought of Elmer gambling.

15. Please sell me a quarters' worth.

16. She is a friend of Janes.

17. The two Negro's faces looked familiar.

18. Fans are looking forward to Kent State meeting with Ohio University Saturday.

19. You must watch your p's and qs'.

20. In the poll there were 42 yes's and 51 noes.

III. In the following sentences, choose the correct word by <u>underlining</u> it. Be prepared to explain your choice.

1. To (who, whom) should the letter be addressed?

2. (Who, whom) will be selected for the chairmanship?

3. Do they know (whose, who's) putting up the money?

4. That is North Texas State's star player, (him, he) with the heavily taped legs.

5. Coach Bryant is removing his star player, (him, he) with the heavily taped legs.

6. Do you remember (who, whom) it was that won the Nobel Prize in 1966?

7. Do you think that (we, us) men can do anything about women's fashions?

8. Garets is the only man here (whom, who) I know very well.

9. It appears to be Douglass (whom, who) was injured in that play.

10. Only John and (me, I, myself) are to blame.

11. (Who, Whom), then, would the tax hurt?

12. He had kind words for all the Republican prospects and promised to support (whomever, whoever) was chosen.

13. One purge victim (whom, who) the President apparently believed was personally innocent of wrongdoing was Amelito R. Mutuck.

14. "I'm interested in this cartoon; I would like to talk with (whoever, whomever) drew it."

15. The court is simply trying to reach a decision about (whom, who) gets what first.

16. Did the messenger say (who, whom) the letter was from?

17. Susan Strasburg arrived at the villa of her father, (whom, who) she had not seen in a long time.

18. Danforth asked Rawlins (who, whom) he was representing.

19. It was William White (who, whom) Mr. Young ousted from the presidency of the New York Central.

20. Patton, the delegate from Morganton, N.C., (who, whom) many think may repeat as low amateur, rapped himself smartly on the chest.

7

Agreement of Subjects and Predicates

EXERCISES

These sentences were taken from newspapers and television broadcasts. Correct the errors you find either by copy editing or by rewriting the sentences. Underline your corrections. Some of the sentences are correct, and you should place the abbreviation *Corr.* in the margin.

1. He is one of the greatest choreographers who has ever lived.

2. The General assumed what was then described as dictatorial powers.

3. The couple has two children.

4. Inside the box was a man and a woman.

5. Absent from the meeting were the mayor and two councilmen.

6. Every fireman in the city, 250 in all, were called out.

7. A total of 650 Eskimos was examined and tested.

8. Only one in four were urgent cases, a group that included cardiacs, asthmatics and those found unconscious.

9. The chairman stated that response to the committee's activities have convinced him that the money for renovation can be raised.

10. Business administration and journalism courses provide the student with good background for work in public relations.

11. Here comes the famous Kilgore College Rangerettes onto the field to perform at halftime.

12. Pacing the United States' show of strength were Arthur Ashe and Clark Graebner.

13. The investigation revealed that none of the team members were involved in illegal endorsements of sports clothing.

14. "There's two knocked out cold on the floor!" the sportscaster shouted.

15. Every one of us have asked that question sometime in our lives.

16. The North Texas State freshman squad, nearly 50 strong, has been preparing for their first encounter with Arkansas University.

17. In an era when many a man and woman leave teaching to go into private industry, Dr. J. R. Woolfe took the opposite course.

18. The school board president indicated that the new school probably would be built in Glendale, since that area's need for new facilities were so acute.

19. High in the press box, observing every play, sit either Grubbs or Curtis.

20. Fire Marshal Dave Bowers said there has been three losses, none of which have exceeded $50.

21. Today there seem to be a million different diets.

22. The Navy announced that a task force, including an aircraft carrier, a cruiser and transports loaded with marines, were steaming southward.

23. The TV panel has to guess the person's occupation.

24. Now comes the Colonels of Kentucky for an 8:05 p.m. encounter at Memorial Auditorium Friday.

25. The mayor and members of the city council extend to all season's greetings, the sign on a downtown street read.

26. Adams said that there was some promising clues to link the car with the one at the fire scene.

27. Another factor behind the rising confusion is the distortions that have taken place when some of the recent scientific findings have been repeated by people who did not entirely understand them.

28. Statistical comparison of the teams indicate that Oklahoma is superior to Tennessee.

29. What other steps can be taken in that direction is being discussed by the steering committee.

30. Each of the Boy Scouts was judged on his camping abilities.

31. A constant stream of refugees were seen passing over the bridge.

32. Each of the three boys were born in a different country in Europe.

33. Neither the Hoosiers' coach nor the players were downcast over the loss.

34. There is still an unpublished play and some other manuscripts among Shaw's effects.

35. Two Hereford cows and a one-day-old calf were found dead in the creek.

36. The jury has brought in a verdict of "Guilty."

37. The debate coach, not the debaters, was blamed for the loss to Arizona.

38. He referred to Tyler, Texas, where two-thirds of the world's supply of roses are grown.

39. That breed of hogs are found in central Illinois.

40. Neither the twins nor Mr. Howard intends to do "a complete fade-out."

41. Four full quarters of "sock-'em-and-rock-'em" football was too much to ask of the 155-pound Washington State fullback.

42. The wind and the rain have subsided.

43. The doctor said there was no unwanted side effects by users of the pill.

44. The County Commissioners Court also differ on Buckheit's recommendations for tighter purchasing control.

45. A group of insurgents in the Western area are plotting an overthrow.

46. "You, not your brother, is to blame for the accident," the judge told him.

47. The main example of such failures were the Greek and Roman empires.

48. "Where is the data you gathered?" he asked.

49. None of the ships was sunk.

50. A few bottles of a sweet-smelling liquid, a love potion, was found on a table.

8
Using Pronouns Correctly

EXERCISES

I. These sentences were taken from newspapers and television newscasts. Correct the errors you find either by copy editing or by rewriting the sentences. Underline your corrections. When you find a sentence that is correct, place *Corr.* before it.

1. Although Drake was not expected to give UCLA much of a battle, everyone got their money's worth when the Uclans barely pulled it out, 85–82, in the NCAA semifinals.

2. Each one of the Miss Teen-Agers were judged on their talent, their personality, and their pulchritude.

3. The couple was married in 1966 and were divorced in 1969.

4. Each team was splitting their ends wide.

5. The North and the South each have six backs and six linemen which have been drafted by the NFL.

6. Everybody in Yankee Stadium was on their feet and screaming for a home run.

7. The Ennis Library has been increasing their stack of books since their move to the new municipal building a year ago.

8. Any one of the three vice presidents is qualified to handle their job.

9. He told James that he was responsible for the error.

10. The Viet Cong have demanded that their captives be released.

11. The losing North Carolina team ate their dinner in silence.

12. Washington and Oregon each have won six games and lost two.

13. The mayor presented Nano Scarborough and myself to the governor.

14. Anyone who wants a personalized license plate should send in their application by April 15.

15. "If any player on this team thinks I'm too strict in regard to training rules, they can turn in their suit right now!"

16. Any one of the national civil rights leaders were available for consultation, according to the Massachusetts Senator.

17. At least three farm products contain this strong fiber, and they can be made into fabrics resembling gossamer silk.

18. It's a first down for South Carolina on its own 28-yard line.

19. Cherry nearly came to blows with Axton after he had protested the nomination of Afelbaum.

20. His proposition will be submitted to the board, and it is likely that most of the members will agree with him.

II. These sentences were taken from newspapers, magazines, and TV broadcasts. Most of the errors are in the uses of relative pronouns. There are also some misplaced relative clauses. Correct the errors either by copy editing or by rewriting the sentences. Underline your corrections. Some of the sentences are correct; place the abbreviation *Corr.* before each of them.

1. The epidemic has struck more than 60 persons, at least 11 of which have died.

2. He distributed the rat poison throughout the barn which he had bought that morning.

3. To the question of whom looked good in the line, Walker replied with a wan smile: "I can't remember all of their names right now, but there were seven of them."

4. The senator pointed out that in September General LeMay had not been named, and that voters could only express a preference for "Wallace's running mate," whomever he might be.

5. One of the constructive things that has come out of the meetings of the delegates is that some of them are determined to eliminate these red-tape obstacles.

6. Who do you think Colorado State's quarterback will be?

7. He refused to state, did he not, whom the new employees would be.

8. The President declined to comment directly on the case of the undersecretary, who the Attorney General says was promoted by his predecessor.

9. There are at least seven men who's integrity is to be investigated.

10. Maurice Stans, who President Nixon chose as Secretary of Commerce, is a colleague from the Eisenhower days.

11. With Dietrich Fischer-Dieskau, famed German lieder singer, was his new bride, Christina Pugell, whom he met during a 1967 U.S. tour.

12. One player who you can depend on to make the NCAA Tournament All-Star team is Willie McCarter of Drake.

13. One player who is sure to be placed on the NCAA Tournament All-Star team is Willie McCarter of Drake.

14. They knew they were probably advancing Kennedy ahead of Sen. Edmund Muskie, Hubert H. Humphrey or whomever else might covet the presidential nomination four years hence.

15. They will seriously consider Erlichman, whom they regard as "a terrific Republican property."

16. Regardless of who is chosen, the majority of board members promise to support him.

17. It was Rod Steiger, Academy Award winner, whom they wanted to meet.

18. He swore that he would see to it that Haldeman "got this important post."

19. The chairman of the Board of Regents is leading the fight over who is going to run the university — the board, the legislature or the student militants.

20. The women's editor plans to poll Philadelphia society on who the new "society queen" should be.

9
Using Verbs and Verbals Correctly

EXERCISES

In these sentences, you will find errors in the use of mood and tense, including errors in the use of *shall* and *will, may* and *might,* etc. Other errors result from the needless splitting of verb phrases and infinitives. Rewrite the sentences to make them read well. Some sentences are correct; place the abbreviation *Corr.* before each of them.

1. The American Party will, according to the most reliable sources, try to exploit the school integration issue of bussing Negro pupils to predominantly white schools.

2. The captured "wet back" told border patrolmen that he lived in Nuevo Laredo.

3. The new salesmen are also, after they have had a four-week tryout, allowed travel expenses.

4. They expected to have drawn a much larger audience for the rally.

5. He charged that the Texas Legislature had on at least two occasions that he could recall invaded the board's right to enact rules for management of the university and to, so far as he could determine, fix salaries of the staff.

6. The city manager would have preferred to have received specific instructions from the council regarding enforcement of the ordinance.

7. The mayor always has gone along, and always will, on the plan for improving Fair Park.

8. The coach was firm. "Griffin, if you don't follow training rules strictly, you should turn in your uniform by the end of the week!"

9. He has told the city manager that he might have three months in which to reorganize the police department.

10. The captain reminded his men, "I told you last night that the North Vietnamese may have pushed us from the village."

11. Jess will be 71 years old in February, you will be 68 in April, and I will be 65 in December.

12. Thompson predicted that by the end of today's session the school measure will be approved. However, if it fails to pass, he said he should resign.

13. The mayor shouted, "Vogel, you never did offer to revise the plan!" Vogel heatedly replied, "You're wrong. I certainly did offer to revise the plan—on at least two occasions!"

14. The commissioner shouted, "Either I shall push this plan through or I shall demand the resignation of every commissioner if the plan fails to pass."

15. He said he sued for divorce immediately after his lawyer advised him to.

16. It is almost six weeks now since the mayor and the city manager have spoken to each other.

17. Being the originator of the municipal center plan, Vogel will be given a testimonial dinner one week after the center is completed.

18. Without declaration of a strike by most of the professional players, golf might have managed to weather the storm and kept its family troubles within the family.

19. Were it not for Vogel's unceasing fight, the new municipal center probably would not have been built.

20. He attempted to promptly get the facts.

10

Using Adjectives and Adverbs Correctly

EXERCISES

In the following sentences, you will find these errors: dangling participles, incorrect degrees of comparison, unnecessary splitting of infinitives with adverbs, adverbs instead of predicate adjectives after linking verbs, misleading placement of limiting adverbs like *only* and *hardly*, hyphens in compound adjectives that precede the nouns they modify, omission or awkward use of articles, and confusion of adverbial and adjectival forms. Rewrite or type the sentences as they should be.

1. On the first flight the astronauts will only be expected to remain aloft for a little more than three hours.

2. A amiable, petite blonde, Janie, told police she was frightened at first.

3. Douglass spotted Kawalick quickly and hurled the football farther than he had ever thrown it. It was an 88-yard play.

4. While sitting on the veranda of the luxurious Istanbul Hilton Hotel on the European side of the Bosporus, the winter's first snow is falling.

5. He returned last January after a six-months tour of the Orient.

6. Reese submitted an ms. of 125 pages as his thesis, in partial fulfillment of the requirements for a M.S. degree.

7. The Washington *Post,* New York *Times* and Louisville *Courier-Journal* were ranked in "the top ten" group of newspapers.

8. Jay Milner's next book will be a historical novel.

9. The male bear appeared to be the fiercer of the four.

10. "You just can't hardly stop Mount from hitting those baskets from outside!" exclaimed the sportscaster.

11. Twilliger had been a patient at the Oaklawn Hospital for the last ten days, following an appendectomy.

12. Due to their aggressiveness, Whitener and Randall have nailed down starting assignments on the team.

13. The Cougars have the big guns to immediately and surely cope with most any type of defense.

14. The injured girl, dressed like a hippie, was awfully ugly. She was reported to be resting easily.

15. As she glanced backwards, she suddenly saw a long legged, well built, bearded man emerge from some bushes about thirty five feet away.

16. Alcindor did a real fancy job retrieving the ball off the backboards in the final 12 minutes, and his goal-shooting was absolutely perfect although he was guarded close.

17. The Pulitzer Prize winner told the Temple University journalism students that they would before too long inherit the responsibility of communicating properly information to the public.

18. "If they play deeply, you should bunt," the coach told his freshmen baseball candidates. He thinks his freshmen squad "is coming along real well."

19. He testified that he was present when two FBI men were shot to death, allegedly by a suspected bank robber.

20. Best known outside the fashion world as "the inventor of the Topless Bathing Suit and the No-Bra Bra," the fact is that Gernreich has been . . .

11

Using Prepositions and Conjunctions Correctly

EXERCISES

Various types of errors in the use of prepositions and conjunctions are illustrated in the following sentences. Correct the errors by rewriting the sentences. If a sentence contains no errors, write the abbreviation *Corr.* before it.

1. It appears that chances are fading that Abe Fortas will be confirmed as Chief Justice of the Supreme Court.

2. They intend to gradually win over the peasants in Latin America and thus become strong enough to surround the big cities and gain control.

3. Around 5:30 p.m. the bailiff notified the judge that the jury had reached a verdict.

4. If he had landed in Cuba, he certainly would have been thrown in jail.

5. It looks like he will have to make two separate broadcasts.

6. Looking neither to the right or the left, Otis rammed squarely through the middle of the line.

7. While Abel had been seriously considered for the role, he was turned down by the director.

8. Baker took the handoff and bulldozed his way within one foot of the goal line.

9. Representative McKissack demanded to know if the bill could be amended so it could be passed in this session of the Legislature.

10. Wilson declared that neither he nor his two colleagues were planning to submit resignations.

11. A stalemate, he explained, is where two opposing forces have become deadlocked.

12. It looks as if the Oregon quarterback was hurt on that last play.

13. Simmons had to admit that his group "had received everything we asked for."

14. The youth said he felt keenly a need and interest in getting a college education.

15. One of the main reasons why Nixon won the 1968 election was because he was able to communicate with the younger voters this time where he failed to reach them in 1960.

16. "It looks like everyone but Kearney, Reilly and I will oppose the new zoning ordinance," Mayor Gibson declared.

17. "I just don't know who will pitch tomorrow's game," Schoendienst said, "so your guess is as good as mine right now."

18. Appearing on the television panel, beside Wes Wise, Marvin Steakley and Jesse Price, were five other candidates for city council seats.

19. Advertisement in San Francisco newspaper:
All-Oak Posture Chairs for Secretaries With Built-in Padding.

20. TV broadcast: Around 30 police were on hand to try and rout the crazed killer out of the building.

21. "Polio vaccine will not do any good if kept in a vial; you have to get it in your system," the doctor commented on the radio broadcast.

22. The chairman strongly denied that he would ask the board's support on the proposal.

23. The man identified himself as an insurance salesman, nevertheless the housewife was suspicious of him.

24. It is a fact that wood does not contract like steel does.

25. He told the judge that he had slept in back of the garage that night.

26. He said his committee would be happy to meet with the commission, providing that sufficient time was given to present its case.

27. The SDS meeting had no sooner opened before cat-calls were heard from the audience.

28. The county judge declared that he differed with Commissioner Price on the matter of allocating road repair funds, and he pointed out that the situation was no different than it was two years ago.

29. Headline: TV Equipment To Be Moved In Auditorium

30. It was clear that the man was suffering physically and from amnesia.

12
What Good
Sentences Require

EXERCISES

I. Can you tell which of these sentences are run-on sentences and which are fragmentary sentences? How would you correct the errors?

1. "We have a lot of speed in the backfield, we have both weight and agility in the line, we have a good passing game," the coach declared.

2. Only one body was found. That of the lieutenant.

3. He admitted that he had made some errors, he said he had worked at too fast a pace.

50

4. "You must keep on believing. You must keep on striving. Trusting in your ability to get the job done," he urged.

5. "We must make every effort to avoid another war," he pleaded. "Because a nuclear war probably would destroy civilization."

II. What is wrong with the punctuation of these sentences? Correct the errors.

1. Outside the hovel it was zero, inside it was just below freezing.

2. When they were not being quizzed or beaten the Pueblo's men were continually subjected to Communist propaganda.

3. A dry climate is good for arthritis, therefore, many doctors advise their patients to go to Arizona.

4. "Shelton has not had a good day yet, so he's about due to show his passing magic today," the sportscaster predicted.

5. Being an only child he was spoiled.

III. Errors in the agreement of predicate and subject in the following sentences resulted from the failure of the writer to identify the *simple* subject and the *simple* predicate. The predicate must agree in number with the subject. What should the correct form of the verb be in each of the sentences?

1. Each of those three fumbles have been converted into touchdowns by the Bears, the sportscaster pointed out.

2. Neither Commander Bucher nor his men was permitted to sit or to lie down.

3. The Syracuse players, as well as the coach, was elated over the victory.

4. TV broadcast: "A troop of Boy Scouts are passing the reviewing stand."

5. He told the store manager that kind of fountain pens were not durable.

IV. Can you tell which kind of sentence — simple, compound, complex or compound-complex — each of the following is? Which clauses are independent and which are dependent?

1. Try to find the answer and to make your report comprehensive.

2. These factions include Averell Harriman, who was put in charge of P.O.W. affairs in the State Department almost three years ago.

3. The report was false, but almost everyone believed it.

4. I intend to pay him back when I get the job.

5. "Actually, I have more patience now than I used to have," the President of Colombia commented, "but I do believe that there are moments when it is necessary to fight or see one's program go down the drain."

13
Sentence Unity

EXERCISES

Read the last part of Chapter 13 in *Grammar for Journalists* in which the types of errors found in this exercise are described; then rewrite the sentences to make them read well.

1. President de Gaulle, in bemedaled uniform, was on hand for President Eisenhower's funeral services, so was the Shah of Iran, Constantine of Greece, King Baudouin of Belgium, West Germany's Chancellor Kurt Kiesinger and dozens more.

2. These sources said the message, sent late Thursday night, showed no hint of compromising the bitter Arab-Israeli dispute.

3. Tatum refused to name his companion or say why someone wanted to burn the wrestling arena.

4. In the finale Lolich returned to win his third straight game, thus the Tigers provided the season's biggest surprise by defeating the favored St. Louis Cardinals in the World Series.

5. The new medical center will be contemporary in architecture and design, will be surrounded by a parking area and will have a complete prescription pharmacy and medical laboratory.

6. The house is falling down and the trees dying.

7. One thing which had at first puzzled officers were the remnants of a charred burlap bag found near the wrecked car.

8. Four members of the committee were asked to resign after they failed to present proper credentials.

9. He declared that they would soon see that all applicants were carefully screened.

10. The winning pitcher was McMahon. He gained sweet revenge over the Yankees. McMahon was wild in the first inning. He walked three Yanks. After that he settled down. And, went on to win in the seventh inning.

11. "What we hope to do," Robbins continued, "is try to arrive at a minimum debit figure they will accept to settle the controversy."

12. Last week Colonel-turned-Premier George Papadopoulos and his fellow junta colleagues gained the ultimate symbol of acceptance. This was the resumption by the U.S. of heavy arms shipments to Greece. Shortly after the coup, the U.S. suspended shipments of heavy weaponry to Greece's NATO-committed armed forces. By so doing, the U.S. hoped to gain leverage over the colonels in order to persuade them to return the country to democratic rule. The effort failed. Meanwhile, political and military developments in Europe have given the colonels considerable leverage over the U.S. The growing naval presence in

the Mediterranean convinced Pentagon planners of the need for a strengthening of NATO's eastward flank...

13. The police arrived just as the two men were having a shootout.

14. Director Michael Gordon said, "We knew we had our girl for 'The Impossible Years' after our first meeting and Christina's first reading."

15. Orr avers that he has never done any real campaigning and never will.

16. The opening statement made by Commissioner Mel Price and the candidate who followed him on the panel were surprisingly similar.

17. The damaged boat began to sink rapidly after it ripped its bottom on a submerged tree trunk.

18. He rounded the corner of the building to find two young toughs mugging a teen-aged girl.

19. Each of the applicants is interviewed for about 30 minutes, then all are given a test.

20. The four wounded South Vietnamese civilians were rushed to the hospital and given instant treatment, but all four died.

21. He denied vigorously that he was neither interested nor concerned about his sister's welfare.

22. The Senator urged his constituents to read all they could on the COPSE report, to study all the points covered in the study, and write their Congressmen.

23. Wise is expected to win an easy victory in Place Five Tuesday. He has conducted the hardest campaign of any of the candidates for City Council.

24. South Vietnam should be able to achieve much faster growth than South Korea did after its war. The experts disagree on just how this growth should be pursued. Some favor a crash program aimed at quick success over a three-to-five-year period in easy-to-reach economic goals. Fishing could be easily expanded even before a peace settlement. There is another body of expert opinion that advo-

cates broader long-range projects . . .

25. Teaching the police candidates karate for self-defense purposes is the first step, and it is an important part of their training.

14
Sentence Coherence

EXERCISES

Rewrite or copy edit the sentences in order to correct errors that violate sentence coherence or clarity. Watch particularly for misplaced modifiers, needlessly split phrases, incomplete or incorrect correlative conjunctions, incorrect pronoun references, and dangling words and phrases. Also correct all violations of parallelism and consistency, such as unnecessary shifts in voice, subject, tense, person and number.

1. Dick Nesbit of the University of Texas at Arlington only missed tying the NCAA record in the 100-yard breaststroke by three seconds.

2. While playing quarterback for Oakland last year, his passing average was 28.2 yards.

3. Driving into the northern edge of Denver, the service station attendant whom we asked for directions proved to be very helpful.

4. She is also an excellent swimmer, plays tennis and likes golf.

5. In the early years, this weekly newspaper publisher did everything from set type to solicit ads to reporting.

6. Many UN delegates believed that the same issue would be raised again when the name of China was presented this year.

7. Doctor Johnson is the only political scientist from Southwestern universities to ever have been appointed to the Institute on Communistic Affairs.

8. The coach told the 1968 U. S. Olympic basketball team that it could, despite being the most underrated team in history, win the championship. And it did!

9. His brother told him that his car had been stolen.

10. McKissack introduced the liquor-by-the-drink bill early in the session, which was promptly passed.

11. Being a rabid anti-Semitic leader, the Congressional subcommittee probably will not invite him to appear.

12. The City Council either will raise the tax rate, or it can cut the budget of every department.

13. Coach Mertes said every player was told at the beginning of spring practice that "we must learn to block first of all."

14. Setting a new Olympic record, Jim Hines of the United States broke the tape one second ahead of Lennox Miller of Jamaica.

15. Services for Dwight David Eisenhower, warrior and President, were to be held Monday in the Washington National Cathedral, the Rev. Edward L. R. Elson, minister of the National Presbyterian Church which Eisenhower attended while President, officiating.

16. Norm Van Brocklin began to listen to his assistants, and the team's morale was improved.

17. The union members were told constantly to vote as a solid unit in each election.

18. The girl was tired, hungry and had a haggard face.

19. The tornado wrecked two barns belonging to Charles Mayhew in Sunnyvale, destroying two tractors, 80 tons of hay and 45 tons of corn.

20. He drew the role of chief interrogator, which displeased other members of the committee.

21. The university trustees face two problems: shortage of funds for maintaining buildings and finding capable faculty members who may be willing to accept lower salaries than those offered in state schools.

22. Three Richardson businessmen were killed Tuesday on Central Expressway in automobile accidents while driving home from work in Dallas.

23. The newly formed organization proposes to finance the new museum by asking for large donations from businessmen and will also go to the man in the street for small gifts.

24. Judge Weinfeld commented that "Corallo had been a bookmaker, gambler, engaged in union activities of a ques-

tionable nature and convicted of a narcotics offense."

25. The chairman walked to the front of the platform, pauses a few seconds for silence, then begins to address the delegates.

26. To become an Olympic swim star, training rules must be observed religiously, the coach told Debbie Meyer.

27. He broke his left leg in a fall last winter, but skiing is a sport he refuses to give up.

28. Football teaches a boy to play hard, to play clean and respect for the value of team play.

29. The governor, a former editor, has always shown great respect and love of the newspaper profession.

30. He charged that the night watchman was either asleep or he was drunk.

31. Jimmy Brown starred for Cleveland for nine seasons, and almost all the NFL's records in rushing were set by him.

32. Sweeping around his right end, a towering Michigan tackle suddenly blocked his path.

33. He had begun to show not only a sullen attitude toward his boss but also his wife and children.

15
Sentence Emphasis

EXERCISES

Rewrite the following sentences to emphasize the major ideas. See that minor details are subordinated in each sentence and that central ideas are placed in positions which emphasize them. Use the active voice in preference to the passive voice; arrange any series in an order that builds to a climax; and employ the devices of balanced sentences and repeated words.

1. Eisenhower sank into a peaceful sleep late Friday morning, dying shortly after noon.

2. One of the biggest gambles in Rockefeller's political life was taking the divorce action.

3. It was clearly shown in the election that the governor's plea for support of the school plan was accepted by a strong majority of the voters.

4. Mayor Jonsson stubbornly stuck to his objective of getting approval of the International Airport, week after week, month after month, despite strong opposition.

5. There is a two-to-one chance that the Scarlet Knights can gallop to victory if the three ailing players can round into shape by game time, the coach predicted.

6. Before he died he had lost his job, his family and his friends.

7. The morning she abandoned her husband and two children in their modest home in South Chicago, Mrs. Sarah Puffer was seen at the High-Tree Tavern and was found stabbed to death at the rear of the tavern three hours later.

8. County Sheriff Bill Decker said Wednesday that the slain woman had written two checks for $2,100 the day she

was strangled to death in her fashionable home in Seagoville.

9. Ten days after Ky and his six negotiators arrived in the French capital from South Vietnam, the important Paris peace talks haltingly began today.

10. The deputy sheriff carried with him a John Doe warrant which he served on the suspected hijacker.

11. A whole block of Elm Street near One Main Place caved in Tuesday and 23 persons were injured, eight critically.

12. In early dealings today the stock market had a broad mixture of gains and losses.

13. The newly elected county commissioner will request the Commissioners Court to raise the county tax rate by at least five cents to provide for establishment of the proposed junior college.

14. Two unidentified burglars, one white and one black, were shot and killed Friday night in the Governor's Mansion — by the Governor himself.

15. Extensive questioning of the suspect got only negative results, as did the polygraph test.

16. Hogs and cattle will be shown in the main barn at the State Fair Tuesday, and a colorful array of exhibits, which will include china painting and ceramics, may be seen in the Woman's Building.

17. When asked to pick the key man on the fine St. Louis Cardinals World Series ball club, Harry Walker's reply was immediate and definite. "I don't like the word 'key,'" declared the manager of the Houston Astros. "A ball club wins as a unit. ... The Cardinals are a well-balanced outfit. But I know what you're driving at," Walker continued. "Every offense has to start somewhere and Lou Brock is the man most responsible for making the Cardinals go at bat."

18. The 81-year-old Negro collapsed on the sidewalk and died an hour later after standing in line all afternoon in the 104-degree heat.

19. Only after a public hearing June 4 will formal approval of the airport plan be given by the City Council.

20. "I've come with Anthony Eden to talk over a few family matters and try to make sure that there are no misunderstandings," Churchill declared on his arrival in Washington.

16
Variety of Expression

EXERCISES

I. Most of the sentences in this exercise were news leads. I have revised most of the sentences to make them less effective than the original leads. Although a majority of straight news story leads begin with a noun, the subject, you should note that the most skillful writers use every opportunity to employ a variety of rhetorical devices to catch the attention of the casual reader. However, in using grammatical beginnings other than the subject, the conscientious reporter will be sure to begin the lead with an idea or a fact which is an important or interesting element of the story. The rhetorical devices, of course, should be used to play up the features in many sentences in the story, not just in the lead.

Rewrite each one of the leads. Be sure to use the grammatical beginning indicated in the parentheses. Remember that the most interesting or important idea should come first. This may be *both* the most important and the most interesting idea.

1. The United States has an official with the title Presidential Counselor—with cabinet rank—for the first time in history. He is Dr. Arthur F. Burns, a noted economist born in Austria who started work at 10 as a house painter. (prepositional phrase)

2. It looks as if the feud between the rural "good roads" bloc and urban mass-transit backers in Congress is about to flare again. It has been a long-smoldering feud. (noun clause)

3. It became inevitable—as days, demonstrations, and riots went by—that President Ayub Khan would have to step down. Most Indians are sorry to see the Pakistani leader go. (adverbial clause of concession)

4. International talks on a solution to the problem of "skyjacking" got under way in Montreal this past week. The 16th skyjacking of 1969 took place as the talks began. (adverbial clause of time)

5. "Can he govern?" That is the question political ob-

servers are asking if, as seems likely, Richard M. Nixon becomes President. (adverbial clause of condition)

6. Sirhan Bishara Sirhan leaped to his feet Tuesday. He pounded the defense table in rage after a state witness suggested he had faked amnesia to mask premeditation in the assassination of Sen. Robert F. Kennedy. (present participial phrase)

7. Industry is donning its deep-sea-diving gear, with more than 1,000 firms already involved in some type of oceanographic work. Industry is armed with a new government report calling for a major national plunge into "hydrospace." (past participial phrase)

8. Today, when baseball clubs slide up and down the standings like runaway elevators, it is an almost impossible undertaking to try to guess in early April who might meet in the October World Series. (gerund or infinitive used as subject)

9. At the finish line of the 100-meter women's track and

field sprint in Mexico City next month, one may find it to be awfully crowded. (pronoun expletive)

10. Barbara Jo Rubin, who is soft, pretty and feminine, didn't look at all like a jockey who had just ridden seven rough furlongs, been beaten on a two-to-one favorite, and heard the raucous boos of the unchivalrous bettors at New York's Aqueduct Racetrack. (adjectival)

11. A three-day occupation of a classroom building at the Newark campus of Rutgers University was ended today. About 30 black students had occupied the building. (adverb)

12. U.S. officials had to dismiss and send home from Mexico City two Negro members of the American team. The reason was that, when they appeared on the winners' stand, they wore glack gloves, gave a Black Power movement salute and bowed their heads when the "Star-Spangled Banner" was played. (adverbial clause of cause)

13. Western foreign ministers are holding a series of meetings in New York this week. The purpose of the meet-

ing of NATO foreign ministers is to answer such questions as what will NATO do if Soviet armies next invade Romania, and possibly Yugoslavia. (infinitive, used adverbially)

14. The U.S. Olympic team showed greatest strength in 1968 in the two sports, swimming and diving, with Charles Hickcox and Debbie Meyer winning three gold medals each. (gerund)

15. The incoming Republican president could collide early with the still Democratic Congress. This could be the case in spite of a pledge from Mike Mansfield to support Richard M. Nixon "when he is right." Mansfield is Senate Democratic Leader. (preposition or prepositional phrase)

16. Atlanta leaders expressed their grief today in the passing of Ralph McGill. They were led by Mayor Ivan Allen Jr. Allen called McGill "the voice and conscience of the South." (past or present participle)

17. Thousands of students went on a rampage from Cairo

to Alexandria. The cause of the trouble was a not-unreasonable decree requiring passing grades for promotion in high school. (causal phrase)

18. Since we are in these days of nudity, peephole pants, see-through blouses, the naked spirit and the bare soul, I find it comforting to cover my head and go sit in the family pew on Easter. (prepositional phrase)

19. Prime Minister Levi Eshkol reached back into his Ukrainian boyhood to sound a note of cautionary wisdom. His statement came shortly after last year's Mideast war, while most of his countrymen were still contentedly contemplating their heady six-day victory over the Arabs. (adverb or adverbial clause of time)

20. Top financial spokesmen of President Nixon told Congress this past week that they intend to halt inflation. They seemed to mean business. They were speaking in quiet tones recommended by President Nixon. (present participial phrase)

II. Try your hand at converting the following poorly written story into a well-written one. Apply all the principles you have learned for obtaining variety of expression. Vary the beginnings of paragraphs and sentences. Try to use all kinds of sentences, long and short, simple, complex and compound, for continued variety. Use some direct quotations.

At 12:03 a.m. Friday Mrs. Lynda Bird Johnson Robb gave birth to a baby girl. The baby weighed 7 pounds, 8 ounces. President Johnson proudly announced the birth of his second grandchild. He did this in an impromptu press conference at Bethesda Naval Hospital.

The President arrived at the hospital shortly after the baby was born, and he greeted his daughter and saw the baby before he met the press.

The President described his new granddaughter as having black hair, apparently being healthy, vociferous, and she seems to know that she is here and has her work cut out for her because she is already expressing herself.

The President, smiling broadly, added that when he saw the baby she was "expressing herself as you females sometimes do."

With President Johnson at the press conference were Mrs. Johnson and daughter Luci Johnson Nugent who came to the hospital with Mrs. Robb at 8:20 p.m. Thursday.

The President happily handed out cigars to reporters; his daughter Luci passed out chocolate candy.

The President said the baby is as yet unnamed.

Johnson said that the father, Marine Capt. Charles S. Robb, was notified of the birth by both radio and cable.

Mr. and Mrs. James Robb, Robb's parents, of Milwaukee, were informed by Luci that they have a new granddaughter.

The President, before leaving the hospital for overnight at the White House, said that pictures of the baby would be sent to Capt. Robb. Capt. Robb is stationed in Viet Nam. . . .

Capt. Walter M. Lonergan, who is Mrs. Robb's doctor, described the birth as normal. And, he added that the labor was uneventful. He stated that he used a regional block anesthesia. Mrs. Robb was in labor at the hospital from 8:20 p.m. until the baby was born at 12:03, the doctor added.

III. Rewrite the following sentences so as to eliminate these faults: stereotyped words and expressions; unnecessary slang; gobbledygook and jargon; circumlocutions (wordiness); provincialisms; colloquialisms; non-idiomatic expressions, including misused prepositions; solecisms and vulgarisms; and failure to use specific, concrete words.

1. Before a host of admiring friends, the couple, wreathed in smiles, were united in the bonds of matrimony.

2. The new department head said that he would try and finalize within the next two weeks a newly routinized program.

3. The coach warned his players that they must face up to the fact that they were about to meet up with a tough, rough team that was in the very pink of condition.

4. The city manager seemed to be bending over backwards to comply to the council's directives.

5. The two bitter rivals battled furiously for possession of

the pigskin in the shadow of the Eagles' goal posts.

6. The people seated in back of us Friday night had quite a little bit of difficulty in drowning out a large 36-piece orchestra.

7. It looks like snow by daylight tomorrow, according to the last KRLD weather forecast.

8. Detectives said they suspicioned that one of the two men was the robber but that they were having to move real slow in their investigation.

9. It was estimated that, providing massive food supplies could not be brought into the region, millions in Biafra might die of starvation.

10. With fear gripping her heart like a vise, the widow woman lifted up the lid on the old, abandoned well and found inside of the well the limp, drowned body of her only child.

11. The crowd waited in breathless silence as the candidate walked very fast to the front of the platform. He imme-

diately and forthwith began to state in a very loud voice that he was the proud possessor of a spotless record, and he pointed with pride to his many achievements during his first term of two years in office.

12. Now the consensus of opinion seems to swing away from the general public and in favor of the hippies, who insist on telling it like it is.

13. When the fuzz arrived on the scene, they found about thirty teeny-boppers and flower children staging a sit-in, in an attempt to get a piece of the action.

14. Crime ran rampant in the Bronx yesterday when gunmen took nearly $35,000 in six separate holdups, and made their escapes, and two teen-age youths were arrested in connection with the shooting of two other youths.

15. The first case of sabotage in a labor dispute between the Donno Company, a private garbage collection concern, and Local 813 of the International Brotherhood of Teamsters, occurred during the night when sugar was poured into

the gasoline tanks of 15 of the company's 33 trucks.

16. Stages, who said he had been a patient in Mercy Hospital for the last ten days, explained to state patrolmen that when he saw the lights of the truck coming towards him, he veered his car sharply to the right and ended up in a rending, grinding crash into the two-story house. The state police estimated that Stages' car suffered $500 damage and that the building suffered about the same amount of damage.

17. "Oh! That putt liked only about a half an inch going into the hole!" the sportscaster said in a highly excited voice.

18. The main issue in the debate preceding the vote, which lasted more than four hours and included several spirited exchanges between two of the Senate's most colorful orators, Mr. Pastore and Senator Everett McKinley Dirksen of Illinois, the Senate Republic leader, was the issue of open housing.

19. The Representative declared loudly that he was not about to spell out inside of the next ten days what type bill he would introduce but that a number of proposals were under consideration.

20. In the first regular noon luncheon meeting of the new party leaders, the main issue in question seems to have been ironed out, and they apparently stood solidly united in their firm resolution to meet the opposition head-on.

17
Punctuation To Make the Meaning Clear

EXERCISES

I. I have removed most of the original punctuation from the following United Press International story and inserted some marks in the wrong places. Correct the punctuation for clarity and emphasis either by rewriting or by copy editing the story.

ABILENE, Tex. (UPI)—Ron Willis is an impetuous young Southern Baptist minister from California whose sideline is getting hippies turned on with Christ.

Willis who prefers not to be called reverend or pastor says he is a street minister.

He has been talking to hippies in Oakland and Los Angeles for two years'. He feeds those who have gone some time with-out meals.

"I chat with them. I dont preach. I feed them if theyre hungry ...

Willis, who is short, and has thick wavy brown hair looks younger than his 28-years. His youthfulness complete with some of the hippie slang and a clerical collar he wears as street minister, are a drawing card for most hippies.

He said the collar worn with an old corduroy coat and shabby slacks "spells help". The young approach him with quiet imploring, calling "Father"? or "Reverend".

It is a person to person ministry that is slow but it is the way the church has to work-on a personal level Willis said.

His brief speech to the Baptist General Convention of Texas in Fort Worth was punctuated with urgings to the staid Baptist leadership to get young people involved in "social gospelism," that gives them usefulness and purpose.

He said work in poverty pockets and ghettos constructing useful habits among the poor was a rewarding outlet for youthful energy...

Willis was in Abilene for seminars and an address to students at Hardin-Simmons University.

Willis discussions in Christian youth groups includes his conversion experience five years ago when he was assistant manager in a ladies ready to wear department in a Sacramento, Calif. store. He says he met a man who "turned him on for Christ.

He tells drug using hippies, "Ive been getting high on God ever since".

Willis said "The hippies have a legitimate search, theyre looking for God; God who loves you even if youre not free white and clean.

"You dont just hand out religious literature and kiss them goodby. You dont just have programs to fill up the long hot summer. Its the long cold winter thats so bad.

Willis tells Southern Baptists if they filled up winter months with youthful activism there would be no long hot summers.

"The church hasnt failed, it just hasnt given enough guide-lines, too many swimming parties and barbecues, and not enough involvement."

II. I have removed most of the original punctuation marks from the following sports column by Bob St. John of The Dallas *Morning News* and inserted some marks in the wrong places. Correct the punctuation for clarity and emphasis either by rewriting or by copy editing the column.

Roger Staubach was going through the paces as the Dallas Cowboy quarterback school opened Monday with a few grunts and groans. Roger Staubach is clear skinned bright eyed enthusiastic, and a picture of health. You seriously wonder if he has heard of air-pollution or it of him.

And he has a crew-cut.

"Something has to be done", said Cowboy publicity director Curt Mosher. "Roger doesnt look like one of our quarterbacks, at least hes got to grow side-burns.

Then Mosher who now often answers himself due mostly to his association with writers said "But . . . sideburns would look funny with a crew cut.

Roger didnt miss a thing Monday and wont during the 2 week 5 day a week school. He had to pick up a rent car Monday after finishing work at the Cowboy practice field. This took time and Roger wanted to get back to the film room, so he said what youd expect him to say. "I'll skip lunch.

Staubach has landed, he is here. Since the Cowboys drafted him after an All America year at Navy he has been somewhat of an enigma a figment. He'd show up at training camp on leave, and then disappear, he had probably been there but nobody knew him well . . .

"He reminds me of Fran Tarkenton", said Ram Coach George Allen. "Except Staubach, I believe has a stronger arm . . .

"Roger will be able to move in quicker," said Coach Tom Landry matter-of-factly. After he's been exposed to the NFL this year he could well be able to do something out there by next year...

Staubach has the enthusiasm of a rookie which only Webster would consider him. He has stayed in good shape; he has thrown plenty; and his arm is as strong as ever...

"Im confident in myself," he said but I'm also realistic, I'm naturally very anxious to find out where I stand."

... "I like Dallas; I like the Cowboys; and this is where I want to play. But again I know I dont have any experience and I have to be realistic. ...

He's been quarterbacking the Navy team at Pensacola...

"We started out real well," added Staubach, "we won six in a row and then lost some players and finished 7 to 2.

Then, Staubach smiled. "We were a passing team, we threw the ball a whole lot. Questioned about this he added "You see I was also the backfield coach.

III. Practically all of the sentences in this exercise were taken from daily newspapers, but most of the original punctuation marks have been omitted and some incorrect punctuation has been inserted. Correct the punctuation errors either by rewriting or by copy editing the sentences.

1. Ruth Eisemann-Schier, first woman to make the FBIs most wanted list for her alleged part in one of the most bizarre crimes of the decade was arrested Wednesday at the Boomerang Drive in where she worked as a car hop.

2. Miss Eisemann-Schier, the object of an intense nationwide search since late December, when she was implicated in the kidnapping of Barbara Mackle the daughter of a millionaire Florida land developer was to be arraigned today.

3. The 26 year old woman who speaks four languages was bewildered when apprehended. "Please excuse me she sobbed before US Commissioner James L. Gullet, "I cant understand all these things; and I would like someone to advise me.

4. The coffin like box was buried 18 inches under-ground, the FBI said. Agents located the macabre subterranean prison in an isolated heavily-wooded rural area some 20 miles northeast of Atlanta Hoover said.

5. The box in which the Emory College junior was buried held an air-pump, food, water, and a battery powered light, that failed just hours before she was located.

6. Hurricane Gladys slashed a path of death and destruction across Florida, from the Gulf to the Atlantic, Saturday; then sped northward aiming 100 mph winds at oft battered Cape Hatteras NC.

7. High above the earth Apollo 7s three chipper Astronauts' continued to orbit flawlessly on their 11 day shakedown cruise to pave the way for an around the moon trip by Apollo 8 in December. Between testing the ships rocket guidance and other systems the crew found time to entertain earthlings with bits of horseplay.

8. Charles Starkweather, who is 20 and a slayer of 11 nurses, won a two weeks stay of execution to-day a little more than an hour before he was to go to the electric chair.

9. The five star general waved from the open window of his third floor hospital room Monday, flashed the V for victory sign and the Eisenhower grin for the bandsmen and waved his small five star flag.

10. A crowd of 69520 frustrated fans saw Baltimores Colts brand the Dallas Cowboys 16 to 10. The Cowboys defense which was burned on the Colt's first play of the game, an 84 yard pass from Unitas to Mackey settled down to play a good game thereafter limiting Baltimore only to field goals.

11. The Northeast Airlines plane carrying 39 passengers, and a crew of three, crashed in a fog and burned 600 feet from the top of 2700 foot Moose Mountain Friday night. 32 died.

12. After eating Carpenter drank the cloudy lifeless wine; and as Carpenter drank tears streamed down his cheeks.

13. A long time militant labor leader she has been shrilly-vociferous about the hammer-and-sickle.

14. Born in October, 1910 in Concord, New Hampshire of Irish American stock she moved to the Bronx with her family 22 years later.

15. Johnson met Bunker; Secretary of State Dean Rusk; Secretary of Defense Clark M. Clifford; and Gen. Earle G. Wheeler, chairman of the Joint Chiefs of Staff, as they arrived at Camp David by helicopter.

16. "I have no statement, I am here to consult with the President," Bunker told newsmen upon his arrival from Saigon. He, then, joined Rusk, Clifford, and Wheeler for the flight to the camp near this town of 3000 people.

17. Archibald, an agent for the National Gas Company will probably it is thought cause a split in the two better

known candidates support in the race for county clerk.

18. James E. Hill, defense attorney for Roberts commenting on Jenkins confession said, "My client will be completely vindicated, he is innocent of the killing".

19. The captain of the Pueblo began to wonder what was going on, so he went forward to the crews quarters.

20. Theyre buying cheaper ones though than they used to, that's why the nations music merchants, here in convention assembled report sales at a $350,000 peak.

21. Matt Dillon firing from his hip blasted his way back to his old position. Later however he tossed the gun away.

22. Before the shooting traffic was halted and the swarming spectators were herded to a safe distance.

23. The trolley lurched and threw Xenia to the floor crushing his nose.

24. As the fire spread the pastor and his wife frantically fought the flames. The fire engulfed the school, the church and the firemen turned their attention to the residences.

25. A revised ordinance, that will permit the city to cut off water service to customers, will be presented to the City Council for action, Monday.

26. In his pick up truck he had five hogs freshly slaughtered.

27. Fire consumed St. Anthony's Hospital today and the mayor of this South Central Illinois community feared the death toll might reach 60.

28. Or, if you prefer a little grease may be applied to the surface of the part.

29. Eisenhower, grinning broadly was on hand at the north portico, the White House's front door to greet Churchill and Eden, when the automobile rolled up.

30. The following officers were elected: Harold Weiss, president, Barney McGrath, vice president, Winnie Weiss, Secretary and Ray Nix treasurer.

31. Wes Wise declared "We'll campaign hard right up to Aug. 28," however he still did not forecast a victory.

32. Warren Agee M.A, PhD, was named president.

33. E. L. DeGolyer, renowned petroleum geologist and oil executive has been elected to the board of directors of Dresser Industries Inc. H. N. Mallon, president announced today.

18
Correct Spelling
is a "Must"
for the Journalist

EXERCISES

I. Write the past form and the present participle form of
each of these verbs:

1. drag	8. omit	15. equip	22. propel
2. slap	9. travel	16. control	23. cancel
3. hop	10. refer	17. benefit	24. model
4. bar	11. begin	18. slam	25. open
5. flip	12. clot	19. wrap	26. commit
6. plot	13. occur	20. fit	27. differ
7. plan	14. offer	21. prefer	28. submit

29. quarrel	35. stop	41. gossip	47. infer
30. regret	36. compel	42. kidnap	48. box
31. develop	37. remit	43. profiteer	49. fan
32. transfer	38. happen	44. romp	50. row
33. dab	39. exhibit	45. prohibit	
34. snap	40. counsel	46. excel	

II. Write the past participle and the present participle of each of these verbs:

1. hope	6. lay	11. shoe	16. notice
2. tie	7. come	12. believe	17. guide
3. pay	8. scare	13. agree	18. advise
4. argue	9. write	14. dine	19. deceive
5. type	10. eye	15. change	20. use

III. Decide which spelling of each word is correct and write the word.

1. beggar or begar	4. noticeable or noticable
2. outragous or outrageous	5. mannish or manish
3. truely or truly	6. judgement or judgment

7. desirous or desireous

8. useable or usable

9. argument or arguement

10. advantageous or

    advantagous

11. deterrent or deterent

12. courageous or couragous

13. loveable or lovable

14. guidance or guideance

15. forcibly or forceibly

16. forceable or forcable

17. lovely or lovly

18. believeable or

    believable

19. regrettable or regretable

20. changeable or changable

IV. Write the third person singular, present tense, of each of these verbs:

1. reply   4. study   7. hurry   10. worry

2. try   5. deny   8. decry

3. tarry   6. carry   9. pacify

V. Write each of these verbs with the suffix *-ing:*

1. lie   3. die   4. rely   5. dye

2. tie

VI. Write the following words, using *ie* or *ei*, whichever is correct:

1. bel — ve	8. n — ther	15. conc — vable
2. s — ze	9. w — ght	16. y — ld
3. c — ling	10. fr — nd	17. front — r
4. l — sure	11. w — rdly	18. counterf — t
5. p — ce	12. financ — r	19. th — ves
6. conc — t	13. inv — gle	20. rec — ve
7. th — r	14. ch — fly	

VII. Write the plural of each of these nouns:

1. woman	9. cupful
2. boy	10. dish
3. Jones	11. contralto
4. sky	12. potato
5. deer	13. tomato
6. radio	14. appendix
7. hero	15. datum
8. kidney	16. crisis

17. box	24. memorandum
18. motto	25. volcano
19. lady	26. mosquito
20. Negro	27. stratum
21. brother-in-law	28. princess
22. lieutenant colonel	29. phenomenon
23. manservant	30. postmaster general

VIII. Write these sentences, using the correct plurals of the words given in the parentheses:

John says that there are three (Harry) on the team this year.

2. How many (m) are there in the word for a note you make to remember something?

3. Did you dot your (i) and cross your (t) correctly?

4. That student uses too many (and) in his writing.

5. Do you think my (5) look like (3)?

IX. Make each of the expressions in parentheses a singular possessive as you write it.

1. (boy) suit
2. (lady) hat
3. (George) boat
4. (woman) coat
5. (fish) fin

6. (Burns) poems
7. (wolf) howl
8. (Peter the Great) reign
9. (princess) train
10. (box) lid

X. Write each of these to make the word in parentheses a plural possessive:

1. (boy) suits
2. (lady) hats
3. (man) coats
4. (fish) fins
5. the (Jones) cars
6. old (wife) tales
7. (child) playthings
8. (princess) maids
9. (fox) tails
10. (witch) prophecies

11. (deer) antlers
12. (boy) and (girl) rooms
13. (sister-in-law) children
14. three (minute) time
15. the two (Charles) reigns
16. (maidservant) wages
17. (thief) loot
18. their (family) ancestors
19. the (Holmes) restaurants
20. the (Frenchman) politics

XI. Some of the following sentences lack necessary apostrophes. Insert the correct marks as you write the sentences. In a few cases, you may need to add an *s* as well as the apostrophe. If a sentence is correct, check it on your paper.

1. Fifty-five dollars worth of phosphate was used.

2. He returned to town two years later.

3. This paper is yours; Harrys is lost.

4. Mr. Thomas house is on the right. The house on the left is the Holmeses.

5. He refused to devote even one minute time to the project.

6. Hamiter & Holcomb Plumbing Company is on River Street.

7. The annual Fathers and Sons banquet will be held Friday night.

8. Mrs. A. K. Oppenheim will review Dickens *A Tale of Two Cities.*

9. The princess gown was designed by our store.

10. Dont you think its too much to ask?

11. The two little girls faces were caked with mud.

12. Dicks boat needs painting, but Charles is ready for racing.

13. The tickets sold for five dollars each.

14. Although he had declared he could do a good days work, he was unable in three days time to show that he could work satisfactorily.

15. Miss Patsy Martin awarded three ribbons to winners in the girls free-style swimming meet.

16. Three hours of rowing brought them close to the lakes shore.

17. He announced there would be a three hour delay.

18. Audrey and Lillian's furs are alike.

19. This is not ours; its someone elses.

20. The Lions program for improving the city was praised by the mayor.

XII. Write the following sentences, selecting the correct word from those in parentheses:

1. The (altar, alter) was illuminated by candlelight from tall candelabra.

2. The committee voted to (censure, censor) the lawyer on two counts.

3. Thistlewait heaved the shot eight inches (further, farther) than Stanivinski.

4. New York University (lead, led) Washington 24-22 at the end of the half.

5. Santee is (likely, liable) to (loose, lose) his amateur standing.

6. The St. Bonaventure (freshman, freshmen) queen will be introduced at the St. Patrick's Day dance.

7. The city council will consider revising the (ordnance, ordinance) at Tuesday's meeting.

8. The (capital, capitol) building drew more than a half million visitors in 1954.

9. The Kansas State scout's (advise, advice) was to go all out with an air attack against the Sooners in the first quarter.

10. New Mexico's (healthful, healthy) climate is, perhaps, the state's greatest attraction.

11. The governor's firm stand on the bond issue has added to his (statue, stature, statute) in the eyes of the voters.

12. A water shortage is (eminent, imminent) in West Texas.

13. The chairman's (prophecy, prophesy) was treated lightly by the majority of the committee.

14. In a pasteboard box placed on the stoop, the couple found a baby girl. She was a (blond, blonde).

15. Judge Harry Stinson appointed a (counselor, councilor) to defend the youth.

16. (Who's, Whose) float is that leading the Homecoming Day parade?

17. The strip-teaser's (sensual, sensuous) movements brought dilatory applause from the night-club audience.

18. Carlton Edwards (formerly, formally) held the post of editor.

19. The old Negro's method of locating a likely (sight, cite, site) for a water well was ingenious to say the least.

XIII. Rewrite or copy edit the following sentences to correct the errors in spelling and in the use of the possessive case:

1. Miss Ott, the defendant, claimed that the gun she held discharged accidently as the two scuffeled after an arguement.

2. One-fifth of the nations' children suffer from poorly aligned teeth, the State Health Department says. The principle causes are persistant thumbsucking and abnormal pressures against the jaws.

3. The marshall was surprised to find that the woman's name was misspelled in the warrent.

4. As an amatuer athelete, he is doing alright.

5. Only one library in any area is eligable to receive a gift of new referance books.

6. With nearly 100 new Federal judgeships dangling in Washington, there are excellent opportunities for a little discrete handshaking and politicing.

7. Mr. Fortas concured and disented with judicial awareness, perspicuity and independence.

8. The free lance found that he could develope the materiel and that it was useable for a saleable feature article.

9. The county commissioner's court findings and recomendations, to be contained in a seperate report, are now in preperation.

10. An embarassed judge ruled that the canon's evidence was not admissable.

11. The sargeant appologised for being unable to give the captian a definate discription of the ambidexterous gunman.

12. She apparantly was exhilerated by her financee's humourous anecdotes.

13. The high school principle imediately disapeared in to his office and preceded to analize the situation.

14. When he checked back on the written copy for the advertizment, he was apalled to find that it was he who had accidently made the mistake in grammer.

15. Freshmen legislators evidentally will call the turn on the election of the next House Speaker.

16. When no desert was served at lunch, one president facetioussly remarked that this was "just one more proof that university presidents are not getting their just deserts."

17. The 1970 Mercuries will have many engineering changes.

18. A tight mound dual between Reed and Pressley was broken up when freshmen Goode tripelled in the nineth inning for a 3-1 victory for the Longhorns.

19. The government official announced that this last year Nevada lead all states in number of divorces granted.

20. The persistant high school journalism advisor told the members of the newspaper staff that they must be conscious of their obligations to the student body. He predicted that the staff would produce a succesful, prize winning paper.

21. It is all together possible that the proffesor's proficicency has not been reconized by the administrater.

22. The workers are usually payed at the begining of the week.

23. On that ocassion the hotels were unable to accomodate at least fourty dissappointed visitors.

24. The confidant defence councillor dextrously parryed each question.

25. She said she was Knights' girl freind at the time the offence occured.

26. "You know its a failing of the "pullbacks" — they dont want to move ahead at all, no matter how desireable such action might be."

27. "No, you cant go out with the hairbrained Archie!" "Oh, Daddy, dont get to excited!"

28. A spirit of optimizm is noticable on the North Dakota University campus, a canvas of the student body revealled.

29. He was eying a lucious blond in the front row of the chorus.

30. The Florida State sophomores invited all freshmen students to the prom.

31. A committee representing the canidates has drawn up a tenative intenerery.

32. Incidently, he testifyed that he planed to committ the burglery Wendsday night but that he changed his plans when he found the superindant of the apartment house was begining to be supicious.

33. We reconize that you have the priviledge of recommending your neice for the post if you feel she is equiped to handle it.

Independent
Study Tests
in Grammar

HAROLD L. NELSON & WAYNE A. DANIELSON

Soon after the publication in 1957 of the first edition of *Grammar for Journalists*, we decided to construct a series of tests based on the book. Our objective was to provide a set of measures against which a student interested in improving his grammatical skills could determine the extent of his progress.

The four resulting tests were published in 1959 at Chapel Hill, North Carolina, in mimeographed form under the title, *Independent Study in Grammar*. Originally standardized on a national basis, the tests have since been used primarily at the University of Wisconsin and at the University of North Carolina. The following colleges and universities participated in the original test administrations in order to establish norms: the University of Oregon, Texas Technological College, Louisiana State University, West Virginia University, Seattle University, North Texas State University, Texas Southern University, the University of Minnesota, the University of Kansas, Los Angeles State College, the University of North Carolina, the University of Washington, the University of Wisconsin, Texas Christian

University, Brigham Young University, the University of Nevada, the University of Missouri, and the University of Iowa.

At Wisconsin, where the tests have been used in an independent study program in grammar, students who appear to need special instruction in grammar are assigned to study *Grammar for Journalists* regularly and are required to take tests periodically on the sections they have studied.

At North Carolina, Test 4 has been used primarily as a diagnostic test in the beginning news-writing course. Students who score low are advised to take a self-study course in grammar or to seek another major. No formal program of instruction in grammar has been set up, however.

Our objective in publishing the tests in this workbook is to make our independent study program more widely available. The tests have been revised and updated. It is our hope that students who follow the assignments and take the tests as suggested will be encouraged to improve their grammar, spelling and punctuation – the basic abilities which every journalist should master. For those students who use the revised *Grammar for Journalists* in more formal class settings, the tests should provide a convenient and useful method to prepare for examinations and to measure individual mastery of the material presented in the text.

Sections Covered by the Tests

Test 1 covers chapters 1–8 and 17–18, and pages 312–317 of the spelling list.

Test 2 covers chapters 5–14 and 17–18, and pages 317–322 of the spelling list.

Test 3 covers chapters 6–14 and 17–18, and pages 323–327 of the spelling list.

Test 4 (Final) covers the entire text of *Grammar for Journalists*.

Each test contains sections on grammar, spelling and

punctuation. The first three tests have 75 items each; the final test has 100 items.

How to Take the Tests

Be sure that you have a quiet place in which to take the tests. Observe the time limits. These are closed book exams; do not attempt to look up correct answers while taking the tests. Score your results carefully by using the answer keys on pages 178-184. Interpret your score by referring to the norms on pages 118-121.

You will find it most beneficial to take the final examination (Test 4) both at the beginning of your course of study and again at the end, in order to measure the extent of your progress. Two sets of Test 4 are provided for that purpose.

Grammatical Skill and Success in Journalism

In the last decade, we have conducted a number of studies to determine what relation exists between grammatical skill, as measured by our tests, and success in journalism courses.

The scattergram in Table 1 shows a typical relationship — that between the total score made on Test 4 by 44 University of North Carolina students in 1962 and their grades in Journalism 53, News Writing. The table demonstrates that making a low score on the grammar test is associated with getting a low grade (C, D or F) in the course; making a high score on the test is no guarantee of getting a high grade in the course, but the likelihood is greater. One might say that grammatical skill appears to be a desirable but not essential condition for success in news writing at the University of North Carolina.

TABLE 1. Relationship between Total Score on Test 4 (Final) and Grades in News Writing: University of North Carolina sophomores and juniors, Fall 1962.

PERCENTILE SCORE ON GRAMMAR TEST

Grade in Course	0	10	20	30	40	50	60	70	80	90	Total
A									2	2	4
B				1	2		1	1	4	12	21
C			2	3	1	1	2	1	2	5	17
D			1	1							2
F											0
Total	0	0	3	5	3	1	3	2	8	19	44

A more extensive analysis by graduate student Warren Nye showing the relation of test scores — in grammar, spelling and punctuation — to grades received in news writing is shown in Table 2. It is apparent from Nye's analysis that *all* parts of the test are important, but that spelling is crucial. Of those North Carolina students who scored at or above the mean on the spelling section of the test, 76 percent earned a grade of A or B in the course. Of those students who scored below the mean, only 45 percent received a grade of A or B. Similar results were obtained when scores were plotted against grades received in the news editing course. But Nye found less correlation between test scores and grades in such content-oriented courses as journalism history and press law. No significant relationship was found when test scores were plotted against students' over-all grade-point averages in the university. But more low-scoring students dropped their journalism major than did high-scoring students.

TABLE 2. Relationship between Part Scores on Test 4 (Final) and Grades in news writing: University of North Carolina sophomores and juniors, Fall 1962 and Spring 1963. "N" represents number of students tested.

SCORE ON GRAMMAR PORTION OF TEST

Grade in Course	Below Mean	At or Above Mean
A or B	55%	69%
C or Below	45%	31%
	100%	100%
N=	31	42

SCORE ON SPELLING PORTION OF TEST

Grade in Course	Below Mean	At or Above Mean
A or B	45%	76%
C or Below	55%	24%
	100%	100%
N=	27	46

SCORE ON PUNCTUATION PORTION OF TEST

Grade in Course	Below Mean	At or Above Mean
A or B	55%	73%
C or Below	45%	27%
	100%	100%
N=	22	51

SCORE ON TOTAL TEST

Grade in Course	Below Mean	At or Above Mean
A or B	48%	77%
C or Below	52%	23%
	100%	100%
N=	29	44

How to Interpret Your Score on the Tests

Here are instructions for using the norm tables which begin on page 118.

1. Find the norm table for the test you have taken.

2. Add up your grammar test score (see answer key, which begins on **page 178**) for the test taken. All correct answers receive one point.

3. Look up your grammar test score in the raw score column of the table of norms.

4. Your percentile score will be found opposite your raw score.

5. Repeat the process for your spelling test, punctuation test, and total test scores.

Raw Scores. A student's raw score on a portion or on all of one of the tests may be interpreted by reference to the mean and to the standard deviation of the test, printed at the bottom of each table. The mean (arithmetical average) of the raw scores on a particular test is found opposite the symbol "$\overline{X}$" in the table of norms. The "s" figure represents the standard deviation from the mean. A quick comparison will show whether the student's score is better or poorer than average. Those familiar with normal curve functions may also get a quick idea of how much better or poorer than average the student is by noting how many standard deviations his score falls above or below the mean. Roughly speaking, if a student's score is half a standard deviation above the mean, he is better than 69 percent of the students who took the test; if his score is one standard deviation above the mean, he is better than 84 percent of the students; if his score is two standard deviations above the mean, he is better than 98 percent of the students.

Percentiles. A percentile score may be easily interpreted. A student who has a percentile score of 75 has performed at a level equal to or better than 75 percent of those who took the test, and worse than 100 minus 75 percent of those who took the test.

Percentiles are more stable, in a sampling sense, as they depart from the 50th percentile in either direction and as "N" (the number of students who took the test) increases. Practically speaking, that means the student should be cautious about interpreting a higher score on a later test as an "improvement" if the percentile change is a small one and occurs near the 50th-percentile point.

Test 1 Norms

Covering chapters 1–8 and 17–18, and pages 312–317 of the spelling test.

GRAMMAR		SPELLING		PUNCTUATION		TOTAL	
Raw Score	Percentile	Raw Score	Percentile	Raw Score	Percentile	Raw Score	Percentile
0	1	0	1	0	1	0–24	1
1	1	1	1	1	1	25–28	3
2	1	2	1	2	2	29	4
3	1	3	1	3	4	30	6
4	1	4	1	4	9	31	7
5	1	5	1	5	13	32	8
6	1	6	2	6	23	33	9
7	1	7	2	7	37	34	10
8	1	8	4	8	53	35	12
9	1	9	6	9	69	36	13
10	1	10	10	10	81	37	15
11	1	11	15	11	94	38	17
12	2	12	20	12	98	39	19
13	3	13	26	13	99	40	24
14	6	14	35	14	99	41	26
15	8	15	43	15	99	42	32
16	12	16	51	$\bar{X} = 8.2$		43	35
17	15	17	59	$s = 2.5$		44	40
18	18	18	68			45	45
19	21	19	76			46	48
20	29	20	83			47	54
21	40	21	88			48	59
22	50	22	93			49	63
23	62	23	96			50	65
24	69	24	97			51	69
25	81	25	98			52	73
26	89	26	99			53	77
27	96	27	99			54	81
28	98	28	99			55	84
29	99	29	99			56	85
30	99	30	99			57	87
$\bar{X} = 22.0$		$\bar{X} = 16.3$				58	92
$s = 4.0$		$s = 4.5$				59	94
						60	96
						61	97
						62	98
						63–75	99

$$\bar{X} = 46.4$$
$$s = 9.1$$

N = 268

118

TEST 2 NORMS

Covering chapters 5–9 and 17–18, and pages 317–322 of the spelling test.

GRAMMAR		SPELLING		PUNCTUATION		TOTAL	
Raw Score	Percentile	Raw Score	Percentile	Raw Score	Percentile	Raw Score	Percentile
0	1	0	1	0	2	0–16	1
1	1	1	1	1	3	17–20	2
2	1	2	1	2	4	21	3
3	1	3	1	3	5	22	4
4	1	4	1	4	5	23	5
5	1	5	2	5	8	24–25	6
6	1	6	4	6	12	26–27	8
7	3	7	5	7	16	28–29	9
8	4	8	7	8	23	30	11
9	5	9	10	9	32	31	13
10	6	10	15	10	46	32	15
11	11	11	19	11	60	33	18
12	13	12	23	12	76	34	19
13	21	13	32	13	88	35	21
14	28	14	40	14	99	36	22
15	39	15	47	15	99	37	27
16	48	16	57			38	30
17	62	17	65	$\bar{X} = 10.2$		39	38
18	74	18	77	$s = 3.1$		40	42
19	84	19	82			41	45
20	90	20	89			42	48
21	94	21	92			43	53
22	97	22	95			44	57
23	99	23	97			45	62
24	99	24	98			46	67
25	99	25	99			47	71
26	99	26	99			48	77
27	99	27	99			49	80
28	99	28	99			50	84
29	99	29	99			51	86
30	99	30	99			52	88
$\bar{X} = 16.2$		$\bar{X} = 15.1$				53	91
$s = 3.6$		$s = 4.5$				54	93
						55	94
						56	95
						57	96
						58	98
						59–75	99

$$\bar{X} = 41.9$$
$$s = 9.4$$

N = 298

119

TEST 3 NORMS

Covering chapters 10–14 and 17–18, and pages 323–327 of the spelling test.

GRAMMAR		SPELLING		PUNCTUATION		TOTAL	
Raw Score	Percentile	Raw Score	Percentile	Raw Score	Percentile	Raw Score	Percentile
0	1	0	1	0	2	0–20	1
1	1	1	1	1	2	21	2
2	1	2	1	2	2	22	3
3	1	3	1	3	3	23–24	4
4	2	4	1	4	8	25	7
5	4	5	1	5	12	26–27	9
6	7	6	1	6	18	28	12
7	10	7	2	7	30	29	14
8	15	8	2	8	43	30	16
9	21	9	3	9	58	31	18
10	27	10	6	10	74	32	20
11	34	11	7	11	88	33	23
12	47	12	11	12	95	34	26
13	56	13	15	13	99	35	30
14	65	14	20	14	99	36	34
15	71	15	27	15	99	37	39
16	79	16	36			38	45
17	86	17	44	$\bar{X} = 8.7$		39	50
18	90	18	54	$s = 2.7$		40	52
19	94	19	62			41	57
20	98	20	68			42	62
21	98	21	76			43	66
22	99	22	84			44	71
23	99	23	86			45	74
24	99	24	91			46	76
25	99	25	94			47	81
26	99	26	98			48	83
27	99	27	99			49	87
28	99	28	99			50	89
29	99	29	99			51	90
30	99	30	99			52	93
						53	95
$\bar{X} = 13.0$		$\bar{X} = 18.1$				54–56	96
$s = 3.8$		$s = 4.6$				57	98
						58–75	99

$\bar{X} = 39.7$
$s = 8.9$

N = 256

Test 4 (Final) Norms
Covering the entire text.

GRAMMAR		SPELLING		PUNCTUATION		TOTAL	
Raw Score	Percentile	Raw Score	Percentile	Raw Score	Percentile	Raw Score	Percentile
0–12	1	0–11	1	0–2	1	14–38	1
13–14	2	12–13	2	3–4	2	39–40	2
15	3	14	3	5–6	3	41–42	3
16	5	15	4	7–8	4	43–44	4
17	7	16	6	9	6	45–46	5
18	9	17	8	10	9	47	6
19	13	18	11	11	13	48	7
20	18	19	14	12	20	49	8
21	25	20	18	13	30	50	9
22	32	21	23	14	43	51	11
23	39	22	28	15	59	52	12
24	46	23	33	16	74	53	14
25	54	24	39	17	86	54	16
26	60	25	46	18	94	55	18
27	67	26	53	19	98	56	20
28	74	27	61	20	99	57	23
29	80	28	69			58	26
30	85	29	76	$\overline{X} = 14.46$		59	29
31	89	30	82	$s = 3.25$		60	32
32	93	31	87			61	36
33	96	32	92			62	39
34	98	33	95			63	42
35–40	99	34	97			64	45
		35	98			65	48
$\overline{X} = 25.00$		36–40	99			66	51
$s = 5.13$						67	55
		$\overline{X} = 25.53$				68	59
		$s = 5.40$				69	64
						70	68
						71	71
						72	75
						73	78
						74	81
						75	83
						76	85
						77	88
						78	90
						79	92
						80	94
						81	95
						82	96
						83	97
						84–85	98
						86–91	99

$\overline{X} = 64.97$
$s = 11.72$

N = 656

TEST 1

Explanation. This test contains items in three areas: grammar, spelling and punctuation. Some items are easy; others are hard. Do your best to answer all items within the 40-minute time limit. There is no penalty for guessing.

Part I. Grammatical Usage

Directions. Read each sentence and decide if there is an error in usage in any of the <u>underlined</u> parts of the sentence. If you find an error, note the letter printed under the wrong word or phrase, and write the letter in the margin. If you do not find an error, write the letter "E" in the margin. No sentence has more than one error. Some sentences do not have any errors.

SAMPLE:

1. Roger, <u>Jane</u> and Henry <u>is</u> coming <u>to</u> the party <u>at</u>
         A   B   C   D

our house.

In this sentence, *is* is wrong. Place the letter "B" before the sentence.

SAMPLE:

<u>The</u> <u>Indian</u> <u>flung</u> his <u>tomahawk</u> at the intruder.
  A   B   C   D

In this sentence, there is no error in any of the underlined words or phrases; therefore, an "E" should be written in the left margin.

Exercises

1. <u>Its</u> up to <u>him</u> to <u>complete</u> the job on time, <u>according</u>
  A   B   C   D
to the contract.

2. A box of <u>tongue</u> <u>depressors</u> <u>are</u> a useful <u>object</u> to have
          A   B   C   D
around the house, according to a report in the AMA Journal.

3. A <u>Winston</u> does taste <u>good</u>, Allerton <u>reluctantly</u>
     A   B   C
<u>decided</u>.
  D

4. The <u>oldest</u> twin was <u>born</u> shortly before <u>midnight</u> on
     A   B   C
Dec. 31, 1834, in the <u>midst</u> of one of the worst snow storms
                    D
of the century.

5. The rose smells <u>sweetly</u>, <u>particularly</u> when it blooms
               A   B
in a southern garden <u>bathed</u> in the light of an early <u>August</u>
                 C   D
moon.

6. "<u>It's</u> <u>she</u>!" Conrad breathed softly as the spotlight
   A   B
<u>illuminated</u> for a <u>moment</u> a hauntingly beautiful face in
  C   D
the crowd.

7. There is no doubt in <u>anyone's</u> mind that Garcia,
                     A
Jacobowsky and <u>him</u> <u>were</u> involved in the <u>incident</u> that
            B   C   D
night at Mike's Place.

8. After the last car <u>sank</u>, only <u>us</u> two men were left
               A   B
<u>clinging</u> to the bridge <u>abutment</u>.
  C   D

9. <u>They're</u> having a lot of trouble with <u>there</u> car in the
     A   B

<u>spring</u> and fall when they change <u>thermostats</u>.
  C   D

10. The city dump <u>smells</u> <u>badly</u> because so many
                    A   B

<u>diseased</u> elm trees are <u>smoldering</u> there.
  C   D

11. He may know a great deal about <u>medieval</u> history,
                                    A

but <u>apparently</u> he <u>don't</u> know <u>anything</u> about how to behave
      B   C   D

at a fraternity dance.

12. Everyone <u>was</u> forcing <u>themselves</u> through the
             A   B

crowded hall, <u>eager</u> to see the <u>theater</u> idol and if possible
                C   D

to meet him.

13. A vast number of <u>seagulls</u> <u>were</u> flying inland that
                  A   B

morning, <u>apparently</u> in pursuit of invading <u>squadrons</u> of
        C   D

locusts.

14. The cougar <u>lay</u> <u>motionlessly</u> on the rock, <u>its</u> muscles
            A   B   C

coiled for the leap onto the <u>colt's</u> back.
                       D

15. The <u>meeting</u> had to be <u>postponed</u> <u>as</u> the <u>president</u>
        A   B   C   D

had the mumps.

16. <u>Its</u> one of the <u>fastest-growing</u> and most <u>profitable</u>
   A   B   C

lines <u>in</u> the entire steel industry.
     D

17. <u>Whom</u> do you think will be <u>eliminated</u> in the
　　　A　　　　　　　　　　　　　　B
<u>semifinals</u> of the golden gloves <u>tournament</u> Saturday?
　　C　　　　　　　　　　　　　　D

18. He was tall, dark, <u>but</u> <u>good-looking</u>, in the <u>lean and</u>
　　　　　　　　　　A　　　B　　　　　　　　　C
<u>hungry</u> <u>tradition</u> of the American West.
　　　　　D

19. "I wonder <u>who's</u> <u>bicycle</u> this is," the <u>patrolman</u>
　　　　　　A　　　B　　　　　　　　　C
mused as he stood at the scene of the <u>mysterious</u> crime.
　　　　　　　　　　　　　　　　　　　　D

20. According to my <u>uncle's</u> will, the automobile will be
　　　　　　　　　A
<u>her's</u> and the <u>colonial</u> <u>furniture</u> at the house will be mine.
　B　　　　　　C　　　D

21. Will was elected chairman by <u>unanimous</u> vote, <u>and</u>
　　　　　　　　　　　　　　　　　A　　　　　B
will officiate only at <u>irregular</u> <u>intervals.</u>
　　　　　　　　　C　　　D

22. Neither of the winners <u>were</u> willing to shake hands
　　　　　　　　　　　　　A
after the <u>disastrous</u> match at <u>Wimbledon</u> <u>last</u> year.
　　　　B　　　　　　　C　　　D

23. The crow is often thought of as a <u>predator; hence,</u>
　　　　　　　　　　　　　　　　　A　　　B
<u>it's</u> function as a <u>scavenger</u> is sometimes overlooked.
C　　　　　　　D

24. <u>There</u> he stands on the bluff, looking <u>moodily</u> across
　　　A　　　　　　　　　　　　　　　　B
the <u>Mississippi</u> <u>toward</u> the lost lands of his ancestors.
　　C　　　　　D

25. <u>She,</u> as well as many others of her sex, <u>do</u> not
　　A　　　　　　　　　　　　　　　　B
<u>appreciate</u> the fine art of <u>wrestling.</u>
　C　　　　　　　　D

26. Nobody is more generous than him, not even my
     A   B   C   D

own father.

27. The bodyguard looked tough; moreover, he was
         A   B   C

really a coward at heart.
       D

28. Everyone in this classroom has to bring their text to
                A   B   C   D

the next meeting.

29. The rules governing women's late hours aren't
         A   B

wrong, but the method of enforcing them should be im-
       C   D

proved.

30. The report shows that one in twelve undergraduates
                                A

are aided by scholarships at this university.
B   C   D

Part II. Spelling

Directions. In some of the following groups of words, one word is misspelled. If you find a wrongly spelled word, note the letter printed before it, and write the letter in the left margin. If you think all four words are correctly spelled, write "E" in the left margin.

SAMPLE:

    A. familiar
    B. cemetary
    C. outside
    D. receive
    E. *none wrong*

In this group of words, *cemetery* is misspelled. Therefore, the letter "B" should be written in the left margin.

Exercises

31. A boundry
    B certain
    C audible
    D bankruptcy
    E *none wrong*
32. A development
    B deceitful
    C allies
    D cheif
    E *none wrong*
33. A argueing
    B barricade
    C belligerent
    D bouquet
    E *none wrong*
34. A bizarre
    B alias
    C align
    D devide
    E *none wrong*
35. A colonel
    B collateral
    C conspicuous
    D domitory
    E *none wrong*
36. A allocate
    B balistics
    C deceased
    D derived
    E *none wrong*
37. A artic
    B champagne
    C conceit
    D countenance
    E *none wrong*

38. A deign
    B captian
    C allegiance
    D basically
    E *none wrong*
39. A concubine
    B cylinder
    C competant
    D appellate
    E *none wrong*
40. A abscess
    B condemn
    C accommodate
    D committee
    E *none wrong*
41. A calk
    B drownded
    C artillery
    D bananas
    E *none wrong*
42. A antecedent
    B antiseptic
    C ascend
    D accidently
    E *none wrong*
43. A aluminum
    B analyze
    C dispair
    D aggressor
    E *none wrong*
44. A across
    B acquire
    C collar
    D beleive
    E *none wrong*

45. A defendent
    B chimney
    C detriment
    D continually
    E *none wrong*
46. A meander
    B alloted
    C consensus
    D autumn
    E *none wrong*
47. A abbreviate
    B bouyant
    C absurd
    D chassis
    E *none wrong*
48. A catagorically
    B depot
    C cooky
    D colossal
    E *none wrong*
49. A equaled
    B battallion
    C basically
    D boisterous
    E *none wrong*
50. A customary
    B contemptable
    C buries
    D chauffeur
    E *none wrong*
51. A courageous
    B cieling
    C camouflage
    D cantaloupe
    E *none wrong*

52. A defeatism
    B copyright
    C begining
    D courteous
    E *none wrong*
53. A accoustics
    B cavity
    C apparatus
    D correlate
    E *none wrong*
54. A asinine
    B descendent
    C brethren
    D detriment
    E *none wrong*

55. A confectionery
    B believe
    C deferred
    D appalling
    E *none wrong*
56. A compel
    B clientele
    C commitee
    D coincidence
    E *none wrong*
57. A debater
    B convenient
    C compatable
    D depth
    E *none wrong*

58. A adviser
    B commemorate
    C commission
    D conduit
    E *none wrong*
59. A admissable
    B antidote
    C careful
    D aggregate
    E *none wrong*
60. A concrete
    B civilize
    C confinement
    D advisible
    E *none wrong*

Part III. Punctuation

Directions. Read each sentence and decide if there is an error in punctuation at any of the underlined points of the sentence. If you find an error, note the letter printed beneath the underlined portion and write it in the left margin. If you think the sentence is punctuated correctly, write the letter "E" in the left margin. No sentence has more than one error. Some sentences do not have any errors.

SAMPLE:

The tough, hard-boiled center began to cry, his leg was
     A   B   C   D
broken.

In this sentence, the comma after *cry* is wrong; it should be a semicolon. So the letter "D" should be written in the left margin.

128

61. It was Apr. 22 before the ice-covered Missouri
         A   B   C
River finally thawed and broke up in the spring of 1855.
      D

62. The executioner, who inherited his rituals from his
                    A
father and grandfather reported only the customary,
                      B
doleful "It is done!" to the commissioner of police.
      C   D

63. In his long, glowing letters to his son-in-law in the
                A   B
old country, Old Jules, the patriarch of the settlement made
                       C   D
the desert seem like an Eden.

64. Knowing nothing, of the terms of the contract, Peter-
                   A   B
kin hesitated; nevertheless, driven by anxiety, he signed it.
             C   D

65. Waters said that the network documentary depicting
hunger among migrant workers did not startle the American
people, it only stirred them momentarily in their "fat, smug
       A   B   C
complacency."
            D

66. The blonde lacked verve, but the brunette had every-
                           A
thing that MGM sought; poise, vitality, figure, beauty,
           B   C   D
carriage.

67. The decade saw a considerable gain in labor unions'
               A
legal rights, he said, but white-collar workers refused to
           B   C   D
organize.

129

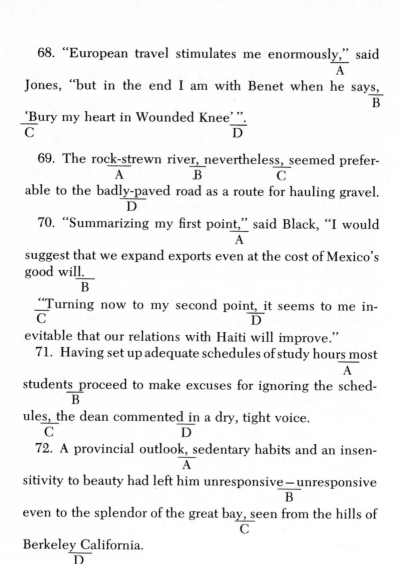

68. "European travel stimulates me enormously," said
                                              A
Jones, "but in the end I am with Benet when he says,
                                                    B
'Bury my heart in Wounded Knee'".
 C   D

69. The rock-strewn river, nevertheless, seemed prefer-
         A   B   C
able to the badly-paved road as a route for hauling gravel.
         D

70. "Summarizing my first point," said Black, "I would
                             A
suggest that we expand exports even at the cost of Mexico's
good will.
      B

"Turning now to my second point, it seems to me in-
 C   D
evitable that our relations with Haiti will improve."

71. Having set up adequate schedules of study hours most
                                                   A
students proceed to make excuses for ignoring the sched-
       B
ules, the dean commented in a dry, tight voice.
 C   D

72. A provincial outlook, sedentary habits and an insen-
                       A
sitivity to beauty had left him unresponsive—unresponsive
                                                  B
even to the splendor of the great bay, seen from the hills of
                                    C
Berkeley California.
        D

73. While it could scarcely be called a "mutt," Unter-
                                        A
baum fel<u>t, t</u>he si<u>x </u>or eight-mont<u>h-ol</u>d puppy had little to
         B   C   D
commend itself to a dog fancier.

74. "No chance for a championship season this yea<u>r,"</u>
                                                    A
the football coach growled at the reporters. <u>"</u>Haven't got
                                              B
the anima<u>ls: </u>no spee<u>d, </u>no weight."
         C   D
75. There was<u>n't </u>much point i<u>n "</u>belaboring the obvious
              A   B
<u>. . . .</u> to the wonder of fools," Martin asserted; and his sub-
 C
ordinates seemed to agree wholeheartedly, nodding vigor-
ous approva<u>l as</u> he spoke.
            D

TEST 2

Explanation. This test contains items in three areas: grammar, spelling and punctuation. Some items are easy; others are hard. Do your best to answer all items within the 40-minute time limit. There is no penalty for guessing.

Part I. Grammatical Usage

Directions. Read each sentence and decide if there is an error in usage in any of the underlined parts of the sentence. If you find an error, note the letter printed under the wrong word or phrase, and write the letter in the left margin. If you do not find an error, write the letter "E" in the left margin. No sentence has more than one error. Some sentences do not have any errors.

SAMPLE:
Roger, <u>Jane</u> and Henry <u>is</u> coming <u>to</u> the party <u>at</u> our
      A   B   C   D
house.
In this sentence, *is* is wrong. Place the letter "B" before the sentence.

SAMPLE:

<u>The</u> <u>Indian</u> <u>flung</u> his <u>tomahawk</u> at the intruder.
 A   B   C   D
In this sentence, there is no error in any of the underlined words or phrases; therefore, an "E" should be written in the left margin.

Exercises

1. Soames opened the control room door, <u>lay</u> the manu-
                                          A
script on the <u>transmitter</u> box, <u>and</u> resolutely seized the
              B   C
microphone <u>and</u> began to speak.
           D

2. The <u>rookie</u> policeman saw that explosives or a sledge
       A
<u>were</u> used to force open the <u>antiquated</u> safe, but he was
B   C
puzzled <u>that</u> no one had heard the burglars.
        D

3. Early results <u>show</u> a sharp geographical split in voting,
                 A
<u>as if</u> the North <u>was</u> objecting to the <u>conservative candidate</u>
B   C   D
and the South approving of him.

4. <u>Raging</u> at "foreigners" and cajoling "you fine American
   A
<u>citizens" in turn</u>, McLong's platform manner <u>struck</u> Annette
B   C
<u>as</u> ludicrous.
D

5. The <u>larger</u> of the chimps <u>raised up</u> to his <u>full height</u>,
       A   B   C
reached for the <u>latch string</u> and pulled it, and opened the
                D
door to the cage.

6. He <u>galloped</u> a horse to Schenectady, drove a team
      A
<u>from there to Albany</u>, and <u>was carried</u> by barge <u>through</u> the
B   C   D
Erie Canal to Buffalo.

7. The great <u>ladys</u> were drawn to Madame Pompad<u>our's</u>
　　　　　A　　　　　　　　　　　　　　　　　　　B
salon when <u>it became evident</u> that she had found the
　　　　　　　　　　C
<u>favor of the king</u>.
　　　D

8. The <u>Martins</u> drove the <u>1,500</u> miles to Atlanta in two
　　　　　A　　　　　　　　B
days, but the <u>Lucases</u> took most of a week, stopping <u>en route</u>
　　　　　　　C　　　　　　　　　　　　　　　　　D
in the Arkansas Ozarks.

9. "The decision is <u>your's</u>," the governor told the finance
　　　　　　　　　　A
<u>committee</u>, "but the <u>comptroller</u> has every right to urge
　　B　　　　　　　　　　C
<u>his opinions on you</u>."
　　　　　D

10. The youth conservation director said that <u>separating</u>
　　　　　　　　　　　　　　　　　　　　　　　　　　A
the girls from inmates of the <u>Womens'</u> reformatory was a
　　　　　　　　　　　　　　　B
necessary beginning <u>in</u> the <u>rehabilitation</u> program.
　　　　　　　　　　C　　　D

11. "If <u>you'll</u> give the long form to Peterson and <u>I</u>, we
　　　　A　　　　　　　　　　　　　　　　　　B
can <u>condense it</u> and make it <u>intelligible</u> to more readers,"
　　　C　　　　　　　　　D
Krautman said.

12. Her parents asked <u>what the occasion was</u>, <u>how long</u>
　　　　　　　　　　　　A　　　　　　　　B
<u>it would</u> last, and <u>with</u> <u>whom</u> she was going.
　　　　　　　C　　D

13. The *Courier-Star* showed <u>an unusual "nose for news"</u>
　　　　　　　　　　　　　　　A

in local reporting, but <u>they</u> didn't require <u>much</u> <u>in the way</u>
                       B   C   D

<u>of</u> good writing.

14. The news staff <u>have</u> <u>uniformly stuck</u> to the goal of
                   A   B

tight writing in the drive <u>against</u> windy reports and
                              C

<u>verbosity</u>.
 D

15. <u>"I'd</u> prefer to send up Monetti," the <u>trainer</u> said,
   A   B

"but <u>120 pounds are</u> <u>just too much for</u> the filly to carry."
         C   D

16. The <u>agricultural</u> reporting service announced in
          A

Aug<u>ust that</u> the best crop in Maine <u>was</u> potatoes, <u>despite</u>
      B   C   D

a rather wet growing season.

17. "Modern plumbing, as well as electrical appliances,
<u>have</u> <u>scarcely reached</u> into the <u>farm slums</u> of northern
A   B   C

Michigan," Drew <u>remonstrated</u>.
                D

18. The survey group found that the <u>high school</u> social
                                        A

studies program <u>was</u> <u>well planned</u>, but that mathematics
                 B   C

<u>were</u> badly taught.
 D

19. The managing editor <u>assailed</u> the kind of <u>an</u> attitude
                         A   B

that lets a repor<u>ter stop</u> digging when <u>he's</u> answered only
                  C   D

those questions about a story that his city editor has asked.

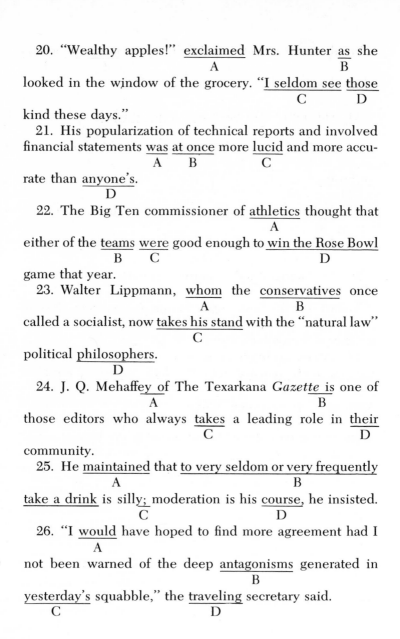

20. "Wealthy apples!" <u>exclaimed</u> Mrs. Hunter <u>as</u> she
                      A   B
looked in the window of the grocery. "<u>I seldom see</u> <u>those</u>
                                       C   D
kind these days."

21. His popularization of technical reports and involved
financial statements <u>was</u> <u>at once</u> more <u>lucid</u> and more accu-
                      A   B   C
rate than <u>anyone's</u>.
          D

22. The Big Ten commissioner of <u>athletics</u> thought that
                                A
either of the <u>teams</u> <u>were</u> good enough to <u>win the Rose Bowl</u>
              B   C   D
game that year.

23. Walter Lippmann, <u>whom</u> the <u>conservatives</u> once
                     A   B
called a socialist, now <u>takes his stand</u> with the "natural law"
                        C
political <u>philosophers</u>.
          D

24. J. Q. Mehaff<u>ey of</u> The Texarkana <u>Gazette i</u>s one of
                A   B
those editors who always <u>takes</u> a leading role in <u>their</u>
                         C   D
community.

25. He <u>maintained</u> that <u>to very seldom or very frequently</u>
       A   B
<u>take a drink</u> is sill<u>y;</u> moderation is his <u>course,</u> he insisted.
C   C   D

26. "I <u>would</u> have hoped to find more agreement had I
       A
not been warned of the deep <u>antagonisms</u> generated in
                            B
<u>yesterday's</u> squabble," the <u>traveling</u> secretary said.
C   D

27. The doctor said <u>that</u> the child <u>always had bled</u> easily
                     A   B
and always <u>would</u>, <u>barring</u> some great medical advance that
           C   D
would help him.

28. The conflict over desegregation <u>exacerbates</u> other
                                    A
tensions in the <u>South</u>, and <u>is driving</u> moderates <u>to cover</u>,
                B   C   D
the lecturer said.

29. "I <u>shall</u> <u>remand</u> the question to the rules committee
       A   B
for clarification," the president said, "unless Mr. Jones
<u>arrives</u> with the necessary <u>data</u> very soon."
C   D

30. Sophomores sometimes <u>get</u> into <u>too</u> many <u>extra-</u>
                         A   B   C
<u>curricular</u> activities, and <u>it</u> often hurts their grades.
D

Part II. Spelling

Directions. In some of the following groups of words, one word is misspelled. If you find a wrongly spelled word, note the letter printed before it, and write the letter in the left margin. If you think all four words are correctly spelled, write "E" in the left margin.

<small>SAMPLE:</small>
   A. familiar
   B. cemetary
   C. outside
   D. receive
   E. *none wrong*

In this group of words, *cemetery* is misspelled. Therefore, the letter "B" should be written in the left margin.

137

Exercises

31. A dilapidated
    B epedemic
    C durable
    D foreword
    E *none wrong*
32. A discernible
    B height
    C frivilous
    D grief
    E *none wrong*
33. A heresy
    B livelihood
    C incidently
    D lingerie
    E *none wrong*
34. A hypocrasy
    B icicle
    C mileage
    D maintain
    E *none wrong*
35. A humorous
    B iridescent
    C menu
    D kindergarden
    E *none wrong*
36. A niece
    B nuisance
    C occassionally
    D incompetent
    E *none wrong*
37. A omission
    B essential
    C efficiency
    D harrass
    E *none wrong*

38. A gnawing
    B except
    C hemorhage
    D genuine
    E *none wrong*
39. A luscious
    B miniature
    C perceive
    D muscle
    E *none wrong*
40. A nickle
    B legislator
    C irrelevant
    D hearse
    E *none wrong*
41. A frivolous
    B extraordinary
    C drunkenness
    D guidance
    E *none wrong*
42. A dilemma
    B distributor
    C gasses
    D mobilize
    E *none wrong*
43. A kimono
    B innoculate
    C incredibly
    D marriage
    E *none wrong*
44. A pastime
    B ninety
    C parley
    D occurence
    E *none wrong*

45. A nowadays
    B moustach
    C khaki
    D lilies
    E *none wrong*
46. A evidently
    B fullfilled
    C hastily
    D digestible
    E *none wrong*
47. A fasinating
    B disease
    C guardian
    D ghost
    E *none wrong*
48. A foreign
    B environment
    C dissipate
    D herald
    E *none wrong*
49. A miscellaneous
    B liveable
    C knack
    D incessant
    E *none wrong*
50. A medieval
    B knuckle
    C parallel
    D naptha
    E *none wrong*
51. A dictionary
    B feasable
    C foresee
    D governor
    E *none wrong*

52.	A fierce	55.	A liable	58.	A Massachusetts
	B handful		B origin		B medicine
	C fragrent		C odor		C pavillion
	D meant		D oculist		D knowledge
	E *none wrong*		E *none wrong*		E *none wrong*
53.	A losing	56.	A monopilize	59.	A messenger
	B managing		B pathos		B maneuver
	C illiterate		C Indian		C marshall
	D jewelery		D intricacies		D myriad
	E *none wrong*		E *none wrong*		E *none wrong*
54.	A exhilarate	57.	A larynx	60.	A gallant
	B freight		B legible		B heredithery
	C grievous		C influence		C listener
	D emphatic		D insalin		D interested
	E *none wrong*		E *none wrong*		E *none wrong*

Part III. Punctuation

Directions. Read each sentence and decide if there is an error in punctuation at any of the underlined points of the sentence. If you find an error, note the letter printed beneath the underlined portion and write it in the left margin. If you think the sentence is punctuated correctly, write the letter "E" in the left margin. No sentence has more than one error. Some sentences do not have any errors.

SAMPLE:

The tough, hard-boiled center began to cry, his leg was
      A   B   C   D
broken.

In this sentence, the comma after *cry* is wrong; it should be a semicolon. So the letter "D" should be written in the left margin.

61. Somehow, Jones thought, he felt more confident
        A   B
since graduation, although it seemed hardly reasonable
that possession of a PhD degree could account for the whole
                C   D
change.

62. "It is you sir, who must explain the difference be-
            A B
tween the budget figures and the yearly expenditures,"
              C   D
Morely said severely to the treasurer.

63. The only survivor of the accident, a dog whose collar
                                 A
bore the name "Rover" sniffed dejectedly at the bodies;
                B   C
then he pointed his nose to the sky and howled.
                                D

64. To recruit a well-balanced freshman team Coach
                A   B
Daniels turned his backfield and line coaches into pro-
     C
moters, sending them to speak at dinners in crossroads
        D
towns around the state.

65. The governor, the mayor and the county supervisor
              A   B
prepared a statement declaring that, "senseless waste"
                                C   D
would be the only result of a referendum.

66. The following officers were elected: William Hol-
                                  A
man, president; Sylvester Tewkes, vice-president; and Miss
  B   C

Marie Ford, secretary-treasurer.
      D

67. The judge said, however, that in one kind of traffic
                  A
case he "threw the book" at the offender; that in which
     B   C
excessive speed was involved.
          D

68. Although garish colors are used on the exteriors of
houses nowadays, architects seldom (and with good
        A   B   C
reason), combine magenta siding and scarlet roofing.
   D

69. Anderson gave a barely perceptible nod—Toby
                                    A
marked it well—in the direction of the door that led to an
                                B
open, sun-bathed porch overlooking the terrace.
 C   D

70. The back to back placement of the chairs and
          A
sofas was a wretched seating arrangement for viewing
 B
movies, but the room could be darkened satisfactorily by
   C   D
pulling the heavy shades.

71. Mrs. Ethelred Smith, 44 of 8236 Sommers Road, was
                   A B
killed when she fell on an open switch-blade knife which
                        C
she had taken away from her 13-year-old son the day before.
                              D

72. The spotlight fell on the striking, dark-eyed blonde,
      A   B   C   D
in the green dress.

73. The senator sai<u>d t</u>hat the meaning of "un-American"
                 A
is no clearer than that of "un-Canadia<u>n"</u> or "un-Frenc<u>h,"</u>
                               B   C
and that he would vo<u>te </u>against the bill.
                      D

74. "The bag of hunters in Wisconsin <u>wasnt</u> quite up
                                    A
to the bag of deer this yea<u>r,"</u> said Smiley. <u>"</u>Some of the
                          B   C
radio announcers sounded kind of disappointed about i<u>t."</u>
                                                   D

75. "The an<u>ti </u>prohibitionists," Mrs. Grundy sai<u>d, "</u>would
              A   B
have our infants imbibing whiske<u>y </u>with their mil<u>k."</u>
                                C   D

TEST 3

.

Explanation. This test contains items in three areas: grammar, spelling and punctuation. Some items are easy; others are hard. Do your best to answer all items within the 40-minute time limit. There is no penalty for guessing.

Part 1. Grammatical Usage

Directions. Read each sentence and decide if there is an error in usage in any of the <u>underlined</u> parts of the sentence. If you find an error, note the letter printed under the wrong word or phrase, and write the letter in the left margin. If you do not find an error, write the letter "E" in the left margin. No sentence has more than one error. Some sentences do not have any errors.

SAMPLE:

Roger, <u>Jane</u> and Henry <u>is</u> coming <u>to</u> the party <u>at</u> our house.
       A   B   C   D

In this sentence, *is* is wrong, Place the letter "B" before the sentence.

SAMPLE:

<u>The</u> <u>Indian</u> <u>flung</u> his <u>tomahawk</u> at the intruder.
 A   B   C   D

In this sentence, there is no error in any of the under-lined words or phrases; therefore, an "E" should be written in the left margin.

Exercises

1. The committee says that the kind of <u>an</u> education it
                                        A
seeks is <u>that</u> which helps students <u>to think effectively</u>, to
         B   C
communicate thought, to make <u>relevant</u> judgments and to
                              D
discriminate among values.

2. The <u>further</u> Thistlewaite moved <u>from</u> the center of
        A   B
the mob, the less he <u>perceived</u> aggressiveness and single-
                      C
mindedness among <u>its</u> members.
                  D

3. The network news director told the <u>audience</u> that
                                       A
he would match his <u>reporters'</u> news sense against any
                    B
<u>newspaperman</u>, and that he'd do so "under whatever
C
<u>circumstances</u> you suggest."
D

4. The singer thanked the old man for the <u>ivory carving</u>
                                           A
that <u>depicted</u> her as Carmen, <u>saying</u> it was the <u>most unique</u>
     B   C   D
gift she ever had received.

5. Wilson <u>contends</u> that it is <u>absolutely correct</u> to count
           A   B
a singleton king as four points under the Goren bidding
system, <u>unless</u> the king is in <u>your</u> partner's suit.
         C   D

6. The effect of a newspaper campaign sometimes is
<u>quite</u> different <u>from</u> that which is hoped for, and <u>many an</u>
A   B   C

144

editor has asked <u>plaintively</u>, "What's wrong with my cru-
                        D
sading technique?"

7. The <u>sales manager</u> suggested to his staff that although
          A
it was <u>alright</u> to criticize "other brands" <u>while demon-</u>
         B   C
<u>strating</u> the new lint remover, it was poor policy to <u>disparage</u>
                                                              D
a specific brand by name.

8. The brothers decided that <u>henceforth</u> they would
                                A
take every precaution to avoid the <u>veterinarian,</u> <u>due to</u> the
                                      B   C
<u>extreme hostility</u> with which he had met them.
      D

9. Because he <u>couldn't</u> hardly see the pavement <u>in</u> the
                  A   B
swirling snow, Bullard stopped the dynamite truck on a side
road, <u>lighted</u> warning lamps, and waited for <u>better weather.</u>
        C   D

10. The <u>scrappy</u> little tackle dug in <u>desperately</u>, but on
           A   B
every charge the opposing line carried him <u>backwards</u> a
                                               C
couple of yards and opened a gap big enough for the half-
back <u>to get through</u>.
       D

11. We <u>only want enough</u> <u>pomegranate</u> seeds for a salad
          A   B
that will serve four <u>persons,</u> but it appears that we'll have
                        C
to buy a pound of seeds <u>unless</u> we're willing to drive six
                            D
miles to Underwood's Market.

12. The <u>exterminator</u> said that he could <u>take care of</u> the
         A   B
rats, but that in a warm, <u>southern</u> climate, <u>to try and</u> rid a
                       C   D
home of every cockroach was "a plain waste of good
money."

13. The true <u>radicals</u> on campus<u>,</u> according to the local
            A   B
newspaper, <u>numbered</u> between 100 <u>to</u> 150 students.
          C   D

14. Carlson got a running start, jumped <u>on</u> the bed of
                                    A
the truck before the <u>vehicle</u> picked up speed, and <u>burrowed</u>
                B   C
under a pile of straw where he lay <u>hoping</u> that he would not
                              D
be discovered.

15. Repaired and <u>refurbished</u>, the Natchez Belle looked
                  A
like a queen while <u>alongside</u> the dock; but <u>under way</u>, she
                B   C
clattered and thumped <u>like</u> she might fall apart.
                    D

16. The heart <u>transplant</u> was a success, according to the
              A
surgeon<u>;</u> the reason why the patient did not survive was
        B
<u>because</u> his <u>kidneys</u> failed.
    C   D

17. The doctor said the fungus <u>that</u> roughens and pits
                          A
the fingernails <u>can</u> be checked <u>rather</u> easily, <u>providing that</u>
            B   C   D
the nails are treated before it advances seriously.

18. A monsoon in <u>southern</u> Asia is <u>when a rainy season</u>
                A   B

146

comes, <u>accompanied by</u> winds from <u>the southwest.</u>
          C   D

19. The <u>stock broker</u> wanted to know <u>if</u> Aanden in-
              A   B
tended to invest <u>for the long term</u> or hoped to <u>make a killing</u>
                         C   D
within a few months.

20. Mrs. Carruthers said that Mr. Foster <u>acted the part</u>
                                               A
of <u>the happy husband</u>, but that just <u>between</u> the girls in
         B   C
the bridge group, she <u>knew better</u> than to be fooled by
                            D
appearances.

21. One Boy Scout was injured and <u>four shaken up</u> when
                                        A
the tower <u>that</u> they had erected in the <u>gymnasium</u> col-
             B   C
lapsed <u>under their weight.</u>
         D

22. The county clerk had thought that when voting ma-
chines came into use in every <u>precinct</u> <u>of the county,</u> <u>that</u>
                                A   B   C
his election-night problems <u>would be</u> solved.
                          D

23. The calculations of the union's executive secretary
<u>contradicted</u> the <u>figures</u> <u>compiled</u> by management and
    A   B   C
printed in the <u>company's</u> house organ.
                 D

24. John <u>later realized</u> that the <u>pensive</u> Maureen had
               A   B
intrigued him because previously he had <u>stereotyped</u> the
                                      C
Irish as gay, outspoken, and <u>with uncomplicated personal-</u>
                                     D
<u>ities.</u>

25. Roberts, the <u>personnel</u> chief, said that the problem
      A
was to discover what <u>was causing</u> discontent <u>among</u> the
       B   C
shipping men and <u>correcting</u> the difficulty.
        D

26. <u>Whatever the inconveniences</u> that might arise be-
      A
cause of the <u>pastor's</u> going, the elder said, the board could
     B
not <u>take offense</u> at his wanting <u>a larger church and congre-</u>
    C   D
gation.

27. While demonstrating <u>on color television</u> the use of
          A
Choco-Cake ready-mix, <u>Martha's thumb</u> was cut by the
        B
electric mixer, and the <u>effect</u> was <u>excruciating</u> for the
        C   D
audience.

28. <u>Noiselessly</u>, he crossed the room on tiptoe and <u>laid</u>
   A   B
the <u>urn</u> on a shelf of the whatnot, where <u>it</u> stood in deep
  C   D
shadows.

29. He offered to resign from the position with <u>whose</u>
              A
<u>extraordinary</u> demands he had <u>coped</u> so well, but the
 B   C
<u>courageous</u> mayor would have none of it.
 D

30. Aside from <u>shockingly bad taste</u>, the article displayed
      A   B
some <u>rather nice</u> qualities, including <u>trenchant</u> expression
   C   D
and careful organization of complex ideas.

Part II. Spelling

Directions. In some of the following groups of words, one word is misspelled. If you find a wrongly spelled word, note the letter printed before it, and write the letter in the left margin. If you think all four words are correctly spelled, write "E" in the left margin.

31. A philosophy
    B pursue
    C preparation
    D quarrel
    E *none wrong*
32. A quandary
    B privilege
    C pneumonia
    D proceedure
    E *none wrong*
33. A typical
    B sophmore
    C ridiculous
    D secondary
    E *none wrong*
34. A quietly
    B reptile
    C reccommend
    D studious
    E *none wrong*

35. A tomatoes
    B superintendant
    C speech
    D rhyme
    E *none wrong*
36. A regard
    B supersede
    C visa versa
    D yield
    E *none wrong*
37. A villian
    B wiry
    C pervade
    D ptomaine
    E *none wrong*
38. A prisoner
    B quarantine
    C seperate
    D referred
    E *none wrong*

39. A shoulder
    B supine
    C tragedy
    D rarefy
    E *none wrong*
40. A zoology
    B tyranny
    C untill
    D vengeance
    E *none wrong*
41. A volume
    B sargeant
    C science
    D rearrangement
    E *none wrong*
42. A procede
    B pretense
    C sauerkraut
    D respectively
    E *none wrong*

149

43. A tied
B solemn
C spaghetti
D rhythm
E *none wrong*

44. A resemblance
B relevant
C seige
D wherever
E *none wrong*

45. A vacuum
B wholly
C simular
D undoubtedly
E *none wrong*

46. A saxaphone
B specter
C wizard
D zodiac
E *none wrong*

47. A verified
B ulterior
C whose
D succede
E *none wrong*

48. A trousseau
B sherrif
C rescind
D switch
E *none wrong*

49. A sororities
B substantial
C spoonful
D tentitive
E *none wrong*

50. A rebellious
B truant
C specimen
D sensable
E *none wrong*

51. A temperment
B strategic
C predominant
D politician
E *none wrong*

52. A partner
B protrude
C trolley
D summerize
E *none wrong*

53. A succession
B referred
C quartet
D quizzes
E *none wrong*

54. A sufficient
B tenant
C scissors
D receive
E *none wrong*

55. A vermillion
B unconscious
C valves
D several
E *none wrong*

56. A rarity
B sheperd
C rheumatism
D strictly
E *none wrong*

57. A platoon
B plaintiff
C specamen
D till
E *none wrong*

58. A schedule
B repentance
C repetition
D reciprocate
E *none wrong*

59. A secondary
B retaliate
C persistance
D quantity
E *none wrong*

60. A pilgrim
B xylophone
C verbatum
D swimming
E *none wrong*

Part III. Punctuation

Directions. Read each sentence and decide if there is an error in punctuation at any of the underlined points of the sentence. If you find an error, note the letter printed beneath the underlined portion and write it in the left margin. If you think the sentence is punctuated correctly, write the letter "E" in the left margin. No sentence has more than one error. Some sentences do not have any errors.

SAMPLE:

The tou<u>gh, h</u>ar<u>d-boiled </u>center began to cr<u>y, </u>his leg was
      A   B   C   D
broken.

In this sentence, the comma after *cry* is wrong; it should be a semicolon. So the letter "D" should be written in the left margin.

Exercises

61. The liberal <u>bloc</u> split down the middle when the sex
                A
education question came before the <u>P.T.A.</u>, but the con-
                                 B
servativ<u>es, </u>true to form, cast a unanimous <u>"no" </u>vote.
     C   D

62. Ortega y Gass<u>et, </u>the Spaniard who wrote "The Revolt
               A
of the Mass<u>es," </u>said that intellectual pow<u>er </u>is measured by
        B   C
<u>its</u> capacity to dissociate ideas traditionally inseparable.
D

63. <u>"You'll</u> never understand 19t<u>h-century </u>Englan<u>d, </u>
    A   B   C
Myrtl<u>e </u>unless you grasp the significance of the industrial
     D
revolution," Miss Prentice lectured her pupil.

151

64. Jasper W. Whipp, grand kleagle of the Hominee
     —————
       A
county chapter thundered, "The time has come to return
              —————   ————
                B   C
to the robes and the torches!"
                        ———
                         D
65. The busy housewife may walk as much as 20 miles
                                            ————
                                             A
a day and never leave her home, furthermore, a lot of that
  ———   ————
   B   C
travel may be up and down flights of stairs.
              —————————
                  D
66. Snow choked the sidewalks, streets and highways
                   —————————
                       A
and buried bushes and park benches, it covered windows
           ——————   ——————
             B   C
and doors of the ranch-style homes in suburban Elmwood
                 —————————
                     D
Heights.

67. The social worker found the little house tremen-
dously cluttered with badly worn furniture, books, clothing
                       —————
                         A
and babies' toys; but the children were reasonably
    ———————
      B
clean and obviously most happy with their pleasant, if
————   ————
  C   D
somewhat untidy, mother.
68. "Is there no possibility," McPheters asked queru-
                 —————————
                     A
lously, "of lightening this stuffy program with just a little
——————
 B C
humor"?
——————
  D
69. The good journalist tries to be objective (unbiased)
                       ——————   ——————————
                         A   B

in presenting news, and perhaps finds it hardest to be objec-
C
tive where he is dealing with causes and effects.
D

70. The inter-American convention of cheese whole-
A
salers was a turmoil of disagreement, the bitterest disagree-
B
ment, undoubtedly, in the history of the event.
C   D

71. They scraped up a hasty, catch-as-catch-can dinner
A   B
from the assortment of canned foods before beginning the
28 mile hike to the trail camp.
C   D

72. "Mrs. Burns," said Hosaki, the gardener, "your
A   B   C
peonies are puny for three reasons, too little sun, too light
D
soil, and too little care."

73. Ale which is practically the same thing as beer to
A   B
many persons, seemed an almost heavenly drink to Jerome,
C   D
who never had been able to stomach beer.

74. "Thirty years ago," said Cox, "nearly everyone knew
A
what the term "twenty-three skiddoo" meant, but today it is
B   C   D
a meaningless relic."

75. "I've never said my goodbye's to that gang before
A   B
without bawling," Marie said as we pulled away from the
C
driveway, "but this time I was really rather glad to leave."
D

153

TEST 4 (Final)

Explanation. This test contains items in three areas: grammar, spelling and punctuation. Some items are easy; others are hard. Do your best to answer all items within the 55-minute time limit. There is no penalty for guessing.

Part I. Grammatical Usage

Directions. Read each sentence and decide if there is an error in usage in any of the <u>underlined</u> parts of the sentence. If you find an error, note the letter printed under the wrong word or phrase, and write the letter in the left margin. If you do not find an error, write the letter "E" in the left margin. No sentence has more than one error. Some sentences do not have any errors.

SAMPLE:

Roger, <u>Jane</u> and Henry <u>is</u> coming <u>to</u> the party <u>at</u> our
      A   B   C   D
house.

In this sentence, *is* is wrong. Place the letter "B" before the sentence.

SAMPLE:

<u>The</u> <u>Indian</u> <u>flung</u> his <u>tomahawk</u> at the intruder.
  A   B   C   D

In this sentence, there is no error in any of the underlined words or phrases; therefore, an "E" should be written in the left margin.

Exercises

1. Among the countrys that fought over feudal claims
          A   B
during the 12th century were France and England.
  C   D

2. He typically won at chess, but checkers were an
       A   B
unfathomable mystery to him.
    C   D

3. Among the 10,000 persons who sometimes lived at
                  A
Louis XIV's Palace of Versailles were hundreds of parasites
     B   C
and hangers-on.
    D

4. Whatever the consequences, he and her must unfail-
            A   B   C
ingly be absolved of all responsibility.
      D

5. The Spanish took the first printing press in North
                       A
America to Mexico City, where it's first issue was a religious
                  B   C   D
work.

6. Armbruster confessed that, unlike most men, he
                           A
actually enjoyed the procession of fads in womens' hats.
  B   C   D

7. In spite of his impulsiveness, Trenton was the man
             A
who the bargemen chose to represent them before the
 B   C   D
commission.

8. Of all the unkempt, ragtag refugees, none looked more
          A   B
disreputable than her.
    C   D

9. Farmer Brown <u>didn't</u> encourage the <u>boys</u> to steal, but
          A   B
he really didn't mind <u>them</u> raiding his melon patch
                       C
<u>occasionally</u>.
     D

10. Every manager and <u>every</u> <u>salesman</u> in the state <u>were</u>
                        A   B   C
instructed to <u>reassess</u> the merchandising program.
              D

11. Arthur Garfield Hays, <u>as well as</u> the famous criminal
                           A
<u>lawyer</u>, Clarence Darrow, <u>were</u> defending Scopes at the
 B   C
"<u>monkey trial</u>" of 1925.
  D

12. All the <u>sustenance</u> that Rivers had during the storm
            A
<u>were</u> <u>cigarettes</u>, coffee and thin barley <u>gruel</u>.
 B   C   D

13. Neither the engines nor the frame <u>were</u> <u>rugged</u>
                                       A   B
<u>enough</u> to <u>withstand</u> the <u>recurring</u> explosions.
 C   C   D

14. He was a success <u>as a sergeant</u> <u>in spite of the fact that</u>
                      A   B
he seldom "<u>chewed out</u>" anyone who didn't shine <u>their</u>
           C   D
boots.

15. Stearns told Botts that in the future <u>he</u> would have
                                           A
to <u>take more care</u> in <u>declassifying</u> <u>apparently</u> unimpor-
   B   C   D
tant papers.

156

16. The large cat began <u>to silently and slowly creep</u> along
                                     A

the <u>limb toward the second crotch</u> where the oriole nest
                    B

<u>hung</u> with its three <u>fledglings.</u>
C   D

17. If <u>everything</u> goes <u>according to plan,</u> I <u>will</u> have
       A   B   C

finished addressing the <u>petitions</u> before the deadline.
                       D

18. Vincent asked <u>whether</u> he <u>might</u> <u>delay making</u> the
                A   B   C

announcement <u>until</u> every board member had seen it.
           D

19. The doctor decided <u>to let Smith rest</u> in the hospital
                      A

for a week, although earlier <u>he had intended</u> <u>to have</u>
                         B   C

<u>operated</u> <u>immediately.</u>
         D

20. The fifth water <u>district</u> control system was <u>more</u>
                 A   B

nearly <u>fool-proof</u> than <u>any other district.</u>
     C   D

21. Martingale, who was <u>real</u> angry at <u>being slighted</u> by
                  A   B

the club, began <u>organizing</u> a scheme <u>of</u> revenge.
            C   D

22. Although not a <u>sympathetic</u> sort, Mrs. Straight
             A

<u>felt</u> <u>badly</u> about backing her car into the <u>children's</u> snow
B   C   D
fort.

23. Grant <u>puzzled over</u> the recessed statues and the
         A

<u>facade,</u> which <u>were</u> water-streaked and <u>sort of</u> ugly.
B   C   D

24. The fruit stand was <u>unattended,</u> but the tramp
                            A
<u>only took</u> <u>a couple</u> of apples and a <u>tangerine.</u>
    B   C   D

25. The bay began to <u>falter</u> late in the day, but the grey
                       A
mare <u>acted</u> <u>like</u> it could keep going <u>all night.</u>
      B   C   D

26. The senator <u>urged</u> that the North <u>try and realize</u> that
                 A   B
its own treatment of racial <u>minorities</u> "is extremely bad"
                             C
in many <u>instances.</u>
         D

27. He said there <u>is</u> <u>to</u> much ignorance of the fact that a
                   A   B
rapidly <u>increasing</u> population strains a state's budget
        C
<u>enormously.</u>
D

28. Understanding <u>relationships,</u> he said, <u>is a matter</u> far
                   A   B
different <u>than</u> merely <u>having</u> a head stuffed with facts.
          C   D

29. He couldn't <u>see</u> <u>where</u> the team would lose any
                 A   B
strength <u>through</u> shifting Chalmers to the <u>guard</u> position.
         C   D

30. Our program for <u>raising</u> money was the only realistic
                     A
one <u>suggested,</u> and the group supported <u>us.</u>
B   C   D

31. Although locked, the old suitcase was <u>coming apart</u>
                                           A
<u>at the hinges,</u> <u>which</u> made it <u>easy</u> to open.
      B   C   D

32. The subjects who sat the plate at the center of the
              A   B   C
sideboard were separated from those who did not.
               D

33. Accidental deaths in Wisconsin were numerous
                 A   B
during the long Labor Day weekend, when 12 persons
drownded and 11 died in traffic mishaps.
  C   D

34. In the old West, vigilante groups often ignored the
                A   B
right to a trial, and sometimes hung a man without even
                           C
hearing his plea.
         D

35. The contestants swum the 50-yard backstroke in
                   A
excellent style, but their times were more than three
      B   C   D
seconds slower than the record.

36. Deliberately, he laid the bits of the incriminating
      A   B   C
letter on a small table while the fascinated jurors watched
                             D
closely.

37. Quentin payed his debts in full; then, almost
          A   B
penniless, he began the promotion that was to make him a
  C   D
millionaire once more.

38. Swinging from the telephone wire, they saw the
                                   A
remnant of a kite's tail and some tattered paper.
   B   C   D

39. The *Journal-Patriot* was an outspoken newspaper, but <u>it</u> <u>didn't seem</u> to <u>care much</u> about getting facts <u>straight</u>.
     A   B   C   D

40. The Optimists Club and the <u>newer</u> group, the Civic
                                       A

<u>Society</u> for Advancing Commerce and Culture, <u>was</u> help-
  B   C

ing <u>in the drive</u>.
     D

Part II. Spelling

Directions. In some of the following groups of words, one word is misspelled. If you find a wrongly spelled word, note the letter printed before it, and write the letter in the left margin. If you think all four words are correctly spelled, write "E" in the left margin.

<small>SAMPLE:</small>
    A. familiar
    B. cemetary
    C. outside
    D. receive
    E. *none wrong*

In this group of words, *cemetery* is misspelled. Therefore, the letter "B" should be written in the left margin.

Exercises

41. A abandon
    B ballance
    C cadaver
    D datum
    E *none wrong*
42. A debater
    B calender
    C bachelor
    D aberration
    E *none wrong*
43. A balloon
    B abhorrence
    C camoflage
    D deceitful
    E *none wrong*
44. A captain
    B defendent
    C bananas
    D abyss
    E *none wrong*
45. A eccentric
    B feasable
    C gauge
    D handful
    E *none wrong*
46. A harrass
    B famous
    C gallant
    D effect
    E *none wrong*
47. A fierce
    B embarass
    C haphazard
    D gases
    E *none wrong*

48. A gnawing
    B February
    C hankerchief
    D economize
    E *none wrong*
49. A identity
    B jaundice
    C kaleidoscope
    D lable
    E *none wrong*
50. A ladies
    B khaki
    C illiterite
    D jealous
    E *none wrong*
51. A judgment
    B knuckle
    C imigrate
    D legislator
    E *none wrong*
52. A kindergarden
    B lavender
    C immovable
    D inaccuracy
    E *none wrong*
53. A magizine
    B nearby
    C oblige
    D pageant
    E *none wrong*
54. A pathos
    B obscene
    C necessary
    D mahagany
    E *none wrong*

55. A nickle
    B occurrence
    C mandatory
    D paralysis
    E *none wrong*
56. A oneself
    B pendulum
    C monstrous
    D neutral
    E *none wrong*
57. A quandry
    B racketeer
    C sacrilegious
    D taking
    E *none wrong*
58. A tariff
    B sherrif
    C radiator
    D quarter
    E *none wrong*
59. A rarity
    B quietly
    C sauerkraut
    D temperament
    E *none wrong*
60. A scissors
    B tentitive
    C realize
    D quarrel
    E *none wrong*
61. A unanimous
    B vaccinate
    C warrant
    D yield
    E *none wrong*

161

62. A zeal
    B weild
    C villain
    D unconscious
    E *none wrong*
63. A varicose
    B useage
    C wherever
    D zephyr
    E *none wrong*
64. A yokel
    B whistle
    C valves
    D utilize
    E *none wrong*
65. A alright
    B bureau
    C article
    D biscuit
    E *none wrong*
66. A concede
    B diagonally
    C dextrous
    D crochet
    E *none wrong*
67. A exorbitant
    B entrance
    C fundamental
    D fragrent
    E *none wrong*
68. A guidance
    B hopeless
    C ghost
    D heroine
    E *none wrong*

69. A itself
    B judicial
    C irrevelant
    D knowledge
    E *none wrong*
70. A loose
    B mobilize
    C lucious
    D muscle
    E *none wrong*
71. A nineteen
    B official
    C outrageous
    D nuculus
    E *none wrong*
72. A positively
    B quantity
    C restauraunt
    D poignant
    E *none wrong*
73. A ptomaine
    B rehearsal
    C rhyme
    D seperate
    E *none wrong*
74. A specialty
    B supercede
    C trouble
    D tenant
    E *none wrong*
75. A utility
    B verified
    C wholly
    D untill
    E *none wrong*

76. A wheather
    B yourself
    C zoology
    D visa
    E *none wrong*
77. A ambiguous
    B built
    C chassis
    D desparate
    E *none wrong*

78. A encourage
    B frivolous
    C greusome
    D hazardous
    E *none wrong*
79. A interfere
    B loneliness
    C menu
    D nullify
    E *none wrong*
80. A overrun
    B prevalent
    C reptile
    D succede
    E *none wrong*

Part III. Punctuation

Directions. Read each sentence and decide if there is an error in punctuation at any of the <u>underlined</u> points of the sentence. If you find an error, note the letter printed beneath the underlined portion and write it in the left margin. If you think the sentence is punctuated correctly, write the letter "E" in the left margin. No sentence has more than one error. Some sentences do not have any errors.

SAMPLE:

The toug<u>h, </u>hard-<u>boiled </u>center began to cr<u>y, </u>his leg was
     A   B   C   D

broken.

In this sentence, the comma after *cry* is wrong; it should be a semicolon. So the letter "D" should be written in the left margin.

Exercises

81. Last <u>night's</u> paper had been use<u>d </u>to wrap the garbag<u>e </u>
        A   B   C
but I found one dated two <u>weeks</u> earlier.
                                D

82. Mrs. Bones tried not to gasp as she viewed her daughter's <u>garb; </u>pointed black shoes, black tight<u>s </u>and skirt,
                A   B
orange <u>lipstick, </u>and bleached yellow hair pulled bac<u>k </u>in
           C   D
an untidy bun.

83. The assistan<u>t </u>who ordinarily is highly efficien<u>t, </u>was
               A   B
<u>all thumbs</u> in <u>today's</u> experiment.
  C   D

84. Nothing could be accomplishe<u>d </u>before <u>Mar. 1</u>, she
                               A   B
explaine<u>d, </u>because bad weathe<u>r </u>would keep the staff
     C   D
indoors.

85. A week later the murder remained unsolved, how-
                                                A
ever, Lt. Holmes's squad had discovered some new clues.
     B   C   D

86. He wasn't much help on the farm that year, he was
       A   B
always off chasing butterflies and looking for birds' nests.
                            C   D

87. Shouting a warning to the crew, Canty ran for the
                          A   B
winch to slacken the tauntly-drawn cable which had begun
    C   D
to hum.

88. The night manager said that he sought a man who had
                       A
four qualities in particular: honesty, imagination, inquisi-
               B   C   D
tiveness and responsibility.

89. "Usually, he wasn't available June, and we had to
    A   B   C
find another helper," Farley explained to the girl.
                D

90. Harvey soberly told the group that, "there's not a
                                    A   B
chance" of repairing the heavily damaged bridge.
      C   D

91. Members of the advisory board were as follows; John
                          A   B
Fox, Miami; Joseph Horn, Denver; and Arthur Block,
                              C   D
Pittsburgh.

92. "If I'm not allowed to go (and I suspect I won't be),
       A   B
I'll just have to make the best of a dull vacation here,"
C   D
Mary said.

164

93. His eyes shifted from the escape valve to the shuttle,
   A   B
and followed its back and forth motion closely.
        C   D

94. The governor's temporary financial adviser, had no
        A   B
time for what he considered stupidity, but was tolerant of
                         C   D
laziness.

95. Twenty five tons of TNT was used in blasting the
      A
300-foot tunnel at the west terminal of King's Highway.
  B   C   D

96. The award went to George Kellers, 17, of 2345
              A   B   C
Heather Drive, who submitted a group of five poems.
            D

97. "I can't find Liechtenstein on this map", said Lovel,
      A   B   C
"but my best guess is that it's near Switzerland."
D

98. Finally grasping Twain's purpose in retelling the
                     A   B   C
story the crowd roared.
     D

99. The Clean Government Society, an organization
                               A   B
opposed to the present city administration will meet
                    C   D
tonight.

100. The Indian ambassador said that Americans
shouldnt expect developing nations to copy the United
  A   B   C
States' economic institutions.
  D

165

TEST 4 (Final)

Explanation. This test contains items in three areas: grammar, spelling and punctuation. Some items are easy; others are hard. Do your best to answer all items within the 55-minute time limit. There is no penalty for guessing.

Part I. Grammatical Usage

Directions. Read each sentence and decide if there is an error in usage in any of the <u>underlined</u> parts of the sentence. If you find an error, note the letter printed under the wrong word or phrase, and write the letter in the left margin. If you do not find an error, write the letter "E" in the left margin. No sentence has more than one error. Some sentences do not have any errors.

SAMPLE:

Roger, <u>Jane</u> and Henry <u>is</u> coming <u>to</u> the party <u>at</u> our
      A   B   C   D
house.

In this sentence, *is* is wrong. Place the letter "B" before the sentence.

SAMPLE:

<u>The</u> <u>Indian</u> <u>flung</u> his <u>tomahawk</u> at the intruder.
 A   B   C   D

In this sentence, there is no error in any of the underlined words or phrases; therefore, an "E" should be written in the left margin.

166

Exercises

1. Among the <u>countrys</u> that fought over <u>feudal</u> claims
         A   B
<u>during</u> the 12th <u>century</u> were France and England.
  C   D

2. He <u>typically</u> won at chess, but checkers <u>were</u> an
       A   B
<u>unfathomable</u> <u>mystery</u> to him.
     C   D

3. Among the 10,000 <u>persons</u> who sometimes lived at
                  A
Louis <u>XIV's</u> Palace of Versailles were hundreds of <u>parasites</u>
     B   C
and <u>hangers-on</u>.
    D

4. Whatever the <u>consequences,</u> <u>he</u> and <u>her</u> must unfail-
                A   B   C
ingly be <u>absolved</u> of all responsibility.
      D

5. The Spanish took the first <u>printing press</u> in North
                             A
America to Mexico City, where <u>it's</u> first <u>issue</u> was a <u>religious</u>
                             B   C   D
work.

6. Armbruster confessed that, <u>unlike most men,</u> he
                                   A
<u>actually</u> enjoyed the <u>procession</u> of fads in <u>womens'</u> hats.
 B   C   D

7. In spite of his <u>impulsiveness,</u> Trenton was the man
                  A
<u>who</u> the bargemen <u>chose</u> to represent them <u>before</u> the
 B   C   D
commission.

8. Of all the <u>unkempt</u>, ragtag refugees, <u>none</u> looked more
            A   B
<u>disreputable</u> than <u>her</u>.
   C   D

167

9. Farmer Brown <u>didn't</u> encourage the <u>boys</u> to steal, but
        A   B
he really didn't mind <u>them</u> raiding his melon patch
                       C
<u>occasionally</u>.
     D

10. Every manager and <u>every</u> <u>salesman</u> in the state <u>were</u>
                        A   B   C
instructed to <u>reassess</u> the merchandising program.
               D

11. Arthur Garfield Hays, <u>as well as</u> the famous criminal
                           A
<u>lawyer,</u> Clarence Darrow, <u>were</u> defending Scopes at the
 B   C
"<u>monkey trial</u>" of 1925.
  D

12. All the <u>sustenance</u> that Rivers had during the storm
             A
<u>were</u> <u>cigarettes</u>, coffee and thin barley <u>gruel</u>.
 B   C   D

13. Neither the engines nor the frame <u>were</u> <u>rugged</u>
                                        A   B
<u>enough</u> to <u>withstand</u> the <u>recurring</u> explosions.
 C   D   D

14. He was a success <u>as a sergeant</u> <u>in spite of the fact that</u>
                      A   B
he seldom "<u>chewed out</u>" anyone who didn't shine <u>their</u>
            C   D
boots.

15. Stearns told Botts that in the future <u>he</u> would have
                                           A
to <u>take more care</u> in <u>declassifying</u> <u>apparently</u> unimpor-
    B   C   D
tant papers.

16. The large cat began <u>to silently and slowly creep</u> along
A
the <u>limb toward the second crotch</u> where the oriole nest
B
<u>hung</u> with its three <u>fledglings</u>.
C   D

17. If <u>everything</u> goes <u>according to plan</u>, I <u>will</u> have
A   B   C
finished addressing the <u>petitions</u> before the deadline.
D

18. Vincent asked <u>whether</u> he <u>might</u> <u>delay making</u> the
A   B   C
announcement <u>until</u> every board member had seen it.
D

19. The doctor decided <u>to let Smith rest</u> in the hospital
A
for a week, although earlier <u>he had intended</u> <u>to have</u>
B   C
<u>operated</u> <u>immediately</u>.
D

20. The fifth water <u>district</u> control system was <u>more</u>
A   B
<u>nearly</u> <u>fool-proof</u> than <u>any other district</u>.
C   D

21. Martingale, who was <u>real</u> angry at <u>being slighted</u> by
A   B
the club, began <u>organizing</u> a scheme <u>of</u> revenge.
C   D

22. Although not a <u>sympathetic</u> sort, Mrs. Straight
A
<u>felt</u> <u>badly</u> about backing her car into the <u>children's</u> snow
B   C   D
fort.

23. Grant <u>puzzled over</u> the recessed statues and the
A
<u>facade</u>, which <u>were</u> water-streaked and <u>sort of</u> ugly.
B   C   D

24. The fruit stand was <u>unattended</u>, but the tramp
⠀⠀⠀⠀⠀⠀⠀⠀⠀⠀⠀⠀⠀⠀⠀⠀⠀A
<u>only took</u> <u>a couple</u> of apples and a <u>tangerine</u>.
⠀B⠀⠀⠀⠀⠀⠀C⠀⠀⠀⠀⠀⠀⠀⠀⠀⠀⠀⠀⠀D

25. The bay began to <u>falter</u> late in the day, but the grey
⠀⠀⠀⠀⠀⠀⠀⠀⠀⠀⠀⠀⠀⠀A
mare <u>acted</u> <u>like</u> it could keep going <u>all night</u>.
⠀⠀⠀⠀B⠀⠀⠀C⠀⠀⠀⠀⠀⠀⠀⠀⠀⠀⠀D

26. The senator <u>urged</u> that the North <u>try and realize</u> that
⠀⠀⠀⠀⠀⠀⠀⠀⠀⠀⠀A⠀⠀⠀⠀⠀⠀⠀⠀⠀⠀B
its own treatment of racial <u>minorities</u> "is extremely bad"
⠀⠀⠀⠀⠀⠀⠀⠀⠀⠀⠀⠀⠀⠀⠀⠀⠀C
in many <u>instances</u>.
⠀⠀⠀⠀⠀⠀D

27. He said there <u>is</u> <u>to</u> much ignorance of the fact that a
⠀⠀⠀⠀⠀⠀⠀⠀⠀⠀⠀A B
rapidly <u>increasing</u> population strains a state's budget
⠀⠀⠀⠀⠀⠀⠀C
<u>enormously</u>.
⠀⠀D

28. Understanding <u>relationships</u>, he said, <u>is a matter</u> far
⠀⠀⠀⠀⠀⠀⠀⠀⠀⠀⠀A⠀⠀⠀⠀⠀⠀⠀⠀⠀⠀B
different <u>than</u> merely <u>having</u> a head stuffed with facts.
⠀⠀⠀⠀⠀C⠀⠀⠀⠀⠀⠀D

29. He couldn't <u>see</u> <u>where</u> the team would lose any
⠀⠀⠀⠀⠀⠀⠀⠀⠀A⠀⠀B
strength <u>through</u> shifting Chalmers to the <u>guard</u> position.
⠀⠀⠀⠀⠀⠀C⠀⠀⠀⠀⠀⠀⠀⠀⠀⠀⠀⠀⠀⠀D

30. Our program for <u>raising</u> money was the only realistic
⠀⠀⠀⠀⠀⠀⠀⠀⠀⠀A
one <u>suggested</u>, and the group supported <u>us</u>.
⠀B⠀⠀C⠀⠀⠀⠀⠀⠀⠀⠀⠀⠀⠀⠀⠀⠀⠀D

31. Although locked, the old suitcase was <u>coming apart</u>
⠀⠀⠀⠀⠀⠀⠀⠀⠀⠀⠀⠀⠀⠀⠀⠀⠀⠀⠀⠀⠀⠀A
at the hinges, <u>which</u> made it <u>easy</u> to open.
⠀⠀B⠀⠀⠀⠀⠀C⠀⠀⠀⠀⠀D

32. The subjects <u>who</u> <u>sat</u> the plate <u>at</u> the center of the
            A   B   C
sideboard were <u>separated</u> from those who did not.
                 D

33. <u>Accidental deaths in Wisconsin</u> were <u>numerous</u>
                  A   B
during the long Labor Day weekend, when 12 persons
<u>drownded</u> and 11 <u>died</u> in traffic mishaps.
     C   D

34. In the old West, <u>vigilante</u> groups often <u>ignored the</u>
                   A   B
<u>right</u> to a trial, and sometimes <u>hung</u> a man without even
                            C
hearing his <u>plea</u>.
              D

35. The contestants <u>swum</u> the 50-yard backstroke <u>in</u>
                   A
<u>excellent style,</u> but <u>their</u> times were <u>more than three</u>
     B   C   D
<u>seconds slower</u> than the record.

36. <u>Deliberately</u>, he <u>laid</u> the bits of the <u>incriminating</u>
     A   B   C
letter on a small table while the <u>fascinated</u> jurors watched
                          D
closely.

37. Quentin <u>payed</u> his debts <u>in full</u>; then, almost
             A   B
<u>penniless</u>, he began the promotion <u>that was to make him</u> a
     C   D
millionaire once more.

38. Swinging from the telephone wire, <u>they</u> saw the
                                A
<u>remnant</u> of a <u>kite's</u> tail and some <u>tattered</u> paper.
     B   C   D

39. The *Journal-Patriot* was an outspoken newspaper,
but it didn't seem to care much about getting facts straight.
  A   B   C   D

40. The Optimists Club and the newer group, the Civic
                                        A
Society for Advancing Commerce and Culture, was help-
  B   C
ing in the drive.
     D

Part II. Spelling

Directions. In some of the following groups of words,
one word is misspelled. If you find a wrongly spelled word,
note the letter printed before it, and write the letter in the
left margin. If you think all four words are correctly spelled,
write "E" in the left margin.

SAMPLE:
    A. familiar
    B. cemetary
    C. outside
    D. receive
    E. *none wrong*

In this group of words, *cemetery* is misspelled. Therefore,
the letter "B" should be written in the left margin.

Exercises

41. A abandon
    B ballance
    C cadaver
    D datum
    E *none wrong*

42. A debater
    B calender
    C bachelor
    D aberration
    E *none wrong*

43. A balloon
    B abhorrence
    C camoflage
    D deceitful
    E *none wrong*

44. A captain
    B defendent
    C bananas
    D abyss
    E *none wrong*
45. A eccentric
    B feasable
    C gauge
    D handful
    E *none wrong*
46. A harrass
    B famous
    C gallant
    D effect
    E *none wrong*
47. A fierce
    B embarass
    C haphazard
    D gases
    E *none wrong*
48. A gnawing
    B February
    C hankerchief
    D economize
    E *none wrong*
49. A identity
    B jaundice
    C kaleidoscope
    D lable
    E *none wrong*
50. A ladies
    B khaki
    C illiterite
    D jealous
    E *none wrong*

51. A judgment
    B knuckle
    C imigrate
    D legislator
    E *none wrong*
52. A kindergarden
    B lavender
    C immovable
    D inaccuracy
    E *none wrong*
53. A magizine
    B nearby
    C oblige
    D pageant
    E *none wrong*
54. A pathos
    B obscene
    C necessary
    D mahagany
    E *none wrong*
55. A nickle
    B occurrence
    C mandatory
    D paralysis
    E *none wrong*
56. A onesself
    B pendulum
    C monstrous
    D neutral
    E *none wrong*
57. A quandry
    B racketeer
    C sacrilegious
    D taking
    E *none wrong*

58. A tariff
    B sherrif
    C radiator
    D quarter
    E *none wrong*
59. A rarity
    B quietly
    C sauerkraut
    D temperament
    E *none wrong*
60. A scissors
    B tentitive
    C realize
    D quarrel
    E *none wrong*
61. A unanimous
    B vaccinate
    C warrant
    D yield
    E *none wrong*
62. A zeal
    B weild
    C villain
    D unconscious
    E *none wrong*
63. A varicose
    B useage
    C wherever
    D zephyr
    E *none wrong*
64. A yokel
    B whistle
    C valves
    D utilize
    E *none wrong*

65. A alright
    B bureau
    C article
    D biscuit
    E *none wrong*
66. A concede
    B diagonally
    C dextrous
    D crochet
    E *none wrong*
67. A exorbitant
    B entrance
    C fundamental
    D fragrent
    E *none wrong*
68. A guidance
    B hopeless
    C ghost
    D heroine
    E *none wrong*
69. A itself
    B judicial
    C irrevelant
    D knowledge
    E *none wrong*
70. A loose
    B mobilize
    C lucious
    D muscle
    E *none wrong*
71. A nineteen
    B official
    C outrageous
    D nuculus
    E *none wrong*

72. A positively
    B quantity
    C restauraunt
    D poignant
    E *none wrong*
73. A ptomaine
    B rehearsal
    C rhyme
    D seperate
    E *none wrong*
74. A specialty
    B supercede
    C trouble
    D tenant
    E *none wrong*
75. A utility
    B verified
    C wholly
    D untill
    E *none wrong*
76. A wheather
    B yourself
    C zoology
    D visa
    E *none wrong*
77. A ambiguous
    B built
    C chassis
    D desparate
    E *none wrong*
78. A encourage
    B frivolous
    C greusome
    D hazardous
    E *none wrong*

79. A interfere
    B loneliness
    C menu
    D nullify
    E *none wrong*
80. A overrun
    B prevalent
    C reptile
    D succede
    E *none wrong*

Part III. Punctuation

Directions. Read each sentence and decide if there is an error in punctuation at any of the <u>underlined</u> points of the sentence. If you find an error, note the letter printed beneath the underlined portion and write it in the left margin. If you think the sentence is punctuated correctly, write the letter "E" in the left margin. No sentence has more than one error. Some sentences do not have any errors.

SAMPLE:

The toug<u>h, </u>hard-<u>boiled </u>center began to cr<u>y, </u>his leg was
　　　　A　　　　B　　　C　　　　　　　　　　　D
broken.

In this sentence, the comma after *cry* is wrong; it should be a semicolon. So the letter "D" should be written in the left margin.

Exercises

81. Last <u>night's</u> paper had been used<u> </u>to wrap the garbage<u> </u>
　　　　　A　　　　　　　　　　　　　B　　　　　　　　　　C
but I found one dated two <u>weeks</u> earlier.
　　　　　　　　　　　　　　　　D

82. Mrs. Bones tried not to gasp as she viewed her daughter's gar<u>b; </u>pointed black shoes, black tigh<u>ts </u>and skirt,
　　　　　　　　　A　　　　　　　　　　　　　　　　　　B
orange lipstic<u>k, </u>and bleached yellow hair pulled bac<u>k </u>in
　　　　　　　C　　　　　　　　　　　　　　　　　　　　　D
an untidy bun.

83. The assistan<u>t </u>who ordinarily is highly efficien<u>t, </u>was
　　　　　　　　A　　　　　　　　　　　　　　　　B
<u>all thumbs</u> in <u>today's</u> experiment.
　　　C　　　　　　D

84. Nothing could be accomplishe<u>d </u>before <u>Mar. 1,</u> she
　　　　　　　　　　　　　　　　A　　　　　B
explaine<u>d, </u>because bad weathe<u>r </u>would keep the staff
　　　　C　　　　　　　　　　　D
indoors.

85. A week later the murder remained unsolved, how-
                                              A
ever, Lt. Holmes's squad had discovered some new clues.
     B C   D
86. He wasn't much help on the farm that year, he was
          A   B
always off chasing butterflies and looking for birds' nests.
                               C   D
87. Shouting a warning to the crew, Canty ran for the
                         A   B
winch to slacken the tauntly-drawn cable which had begun
     C   D
to hum.
88. The night manager said that he sought a man who had
                       A
four qualities in particular: honesty, imagination, inquisi-
              B   C   D
tiveness and responsibility.
89. "Usually, he wasn't available June, and we had to
    A   B   C
find another helper," Farley explained to the girl.
                  D
90. Harvey soberly told the group that, "there's not a
                                    A   B
chance" of repairing the heavily damaged bridge.
       C   D
91. Members of the advisory board were as follows; John
                            A   B
Fox, Miami; Joseph Horn, Denver; and Arthur Block,
                                C   D
Pittsburgh.
92. "If I'm not allowed to go (and I suspect I won't be),
        A   B
I'll just have to make the best of a dull vacation here,"
C   D
Mary said.

93. His eyes shifted from the escape valve to the shuttle,
                                    A   B
and followed its back and forth motion closely.
               C   D

94. The governor's temporary financial adviser, had no
          A   B
time for what he considered stupidity, but was tolerant of
                            C   D
laziness.

95. Twenty five tons of TNT was used in blasting the
       A
300-foot tunnel at the west terminal of King's Highway.
   B   C   D

96. The award went to George Kellers, 17, of 2345
                      A   B   C
Heather Drive, who submitted a group of five poems.
             D

97. "I can't find Liechtenstein on this map", said Lovel,
        A   B   C
"but my best guess is that it's near Switzerland."
D

98. Finally grasping Twain's purpose in retelling the
                        A   B   C
story the crowd roared.
     D

99. The Clean Government Society, an organization
                                A   B
opposed to the present city administration will meet
                       C   D
tonight.

100. The Indian ambassador said that Americans
shouldnt expect developing nations to copy the United
   A   B   C
States' economic institutions.
   D

TEST ANSWER KEYS

You are urged to score your test results carefully by using these answer keys to all four tests, including the final examination (Test 4). Remember that you will do well to take Test 4 both at the beginning of your course of study and again at the end in order to measure the extent of your progress. Two sets of Test 4 are provided for that purpose. You can interpret your score by referring to the tables of norms which begin on page 118.

You will find that the test answers are keyed to the revised *Grammar for Journalists* according to page numbers. You should be sure to check each reference when you find you have made an error. Only by so doing can you expect to avoid making the same error in the future.

TEST 1 ANSWER KEYS

Test 1 covers chapters 1–8 and 17–18, and pages 312–317 of the spelling list.

Part I. Grammatical Usage

	Correct Letter	Page Number(s)		Correct Letter	Page Number(s)
1.	A	32	12.	B	118–19
2.	C	104–105	13.	E	103
3.	E	153	14.	B	58–59
4.	A	37	15.	C	47
5.	A	58	16.	A	32
6.	E	58	17.	A	34, 92–93
7.	B	32	18.	A	45, 173
8.	B	32	19.	A	34, 96, 118
9.	B	330	20.	B	32
10.	B	59	21.	B	45–46
11.	C	111			(*however* or *but*)

	Correct Letter	Page Number(s)		Correct Letter	Page Number(s)
22.	A	114	27.	C	18, 46
23.	C	32	28.	D	118–19
24.	E	– – –	29.	E	– – –
25.	B	104	30.	B	104–105
26.	D	93			

Part II. Spelling

31. A 32. D 33. A 34. D 35. D 36. B 37. A 38. B 39. C 40. E
41. B 42. D 43. C 44. D 45. A 46. B 47. B 48. A 49. B 50. B
51. B 52. C 53. A 54. B 55. E 56. C 57. C 58. E 59. A 60. D

Part III. Punctuation

	Correct Letter	Page Number(s)		Correct Letter	Page Number(s)
61.	A	280–81	68.	D	295–96
62.	B	284	69.	D	300
63.	D	285	70.	B	296
64.	A	unnecessary comma	71.	A	288
			72.	D	287
65.	A	292–93	73.	C	300
66.	C	use colon or dash	74.	E	– – –
67.	E	unless want direct quote	75.	C	281

TEST 2 ANSWER KEYS

Test 2 covers chapters 5–9 and 17–18, and pages 317–322 of the spelling list.

Part I. Grammatical Usage

	Correct Letter	Page Number(s)		Correct Letter	Page Number(s)
1.	A	70	15.	C	104
2.	B	175	16.	E	105
3.	C	74 (could use *was*)	17.	A	104
			18.	D	105
4.	A, B	77, 160 (dangling part.)	19.	B	149
			20.	D	107
			21.	D	113–114
5.	B	68, 71	22.	C	114
6.	C	73, 225	23.	E	94
7.	A	82	24.	C	119
8.	E	82	25.	B	132
9.	A	32	26.	E	140–41
10.	B	91	27.	C	138
11.	B	95	28.	C	138
12.	E	94	29.	E	139–40
13.	B	(*it*, not *they*)	30.	D	123–24
14.	A	103–104			

Part II. Spelling

31. E 32. D 33. B 34. C 35. B 36. C 37. A 38. C 39. E 40. C
41. B 42. A 43. E 44. C 45. C 46. A 47. D 48. B 49. D 50. D
51. A 52. D 53. E 54. D 55. A 56. B 57. C 58. E 59. C 60. C

Part III. Punctuation

	Correct Letter	Page Number(s)		Correct Letter	Page Number(s)
61.	C	280	69.	E	– – –
62.	A	287	70.	A	300
63.	B	285–86	71.	B	287
64.	B	288	72.	D	comma not needed
65.	C	291–92			
66.	E	– – –	73.	E	– – –
67.	C	285–86	74.	A	295
68.	D	comma not needed	75.	A	301

TEST 3 ANSWER KEYS

Test 3 covers chapters 10–14 and 17–18, and pages 323–327 of the spelling list.

Part I. Grammatical Usage

	Correct Letter	Page Number(s)		Correct Letter	Page Number(s)
1.	A	149	8.	C	158
2.	A	150	9.	A	158
3.	C	194 – that of any news-papermen (pl.)	10.	C	158
			11.	A	209
			12.	D	167–68
			13.	D	301
4.	D	152	14.	A	169
5.	B	152	15.	D	166–67
6.	E	156	16.	C	177
7.	B	158	17.	D	178

	Correct Letter	Page Number(s)		Correct Letter	Page Number(s)
18.	B	177	25.	D	223–24
19.	B	178 (*whether* preferred)	26.	E	– – –
			27.	B	211–12
20.	C	168	28.	D	217
21.	A	191	29.	E	*whose* (inanimate usually preferred)
22.	C	193			
23.	E	– – –			
24.	D	223–24	30.	E	– – –

Part II. Spelling

31. E 32. D 33. B 34. C 35. B 36. C 37. A 38. C 39. E 40. C
41. B 42. A 43. E 44. C 45. C 46. A 47. D 48. B 49. D 50. D
51. A 52. D 53. E 54. D 55. A 56. B 57. C 58. E 59. C 60. C

Part III. Punctuation

	Correct Letter	Page Number(s)		Correct Letter	Page Number(s)
61.	B	281	69.	E	– – –
62.	E	– – –	70.	B	299
63.	D	287	71.	C	300
64.	B	285	72.	D	294
65.	C	293	73.	A	284
66.	C	292–93	74.	C	296
67.	E	– – –	75.	A	85
68.	D	295–96			

TEST 4 ANSWER KEYS

Test 4 (Final Exam) covers all chapters in Grammar for Journalists.

Part I. Grammatical Usage

	Correct Letter	Page Number(s)		Correct Letter	Page Number(s)
1.	A	82	21.	A	153
2.	B	105	22.	C	57, 153
3.	E	– – –	23.	D	155
4.	C	86	24.	B	209
5.	B	90, 96	25.	C	166–67
6.	D	91	26.	B	167–68
7.	B	94, 115–16 122	27.	B	155, 168
			28.	C	156
8.	D	93	29.	B	177
9.	C	80, 96, 171	30.	D	123–24
10.	C	156	31.	C	"making it easy to open"
11.	C	104			
12.	B	105	32.	B	70
13.	A	103	33.	C	317
14.	D	119	34.	C	68
15.	A	123–24	35.	A	69
16.	A	131–32	36.	E	– – –
17.	E	139–40 (*shall* or *will*)	37.	A	68
			38.	A	160, 219
18.	E	178	39.	E	– – –
19.	C	137	40.	C	101
20.	D	"than that of" or "any other district's"			

Part II. Spelling

41. B 42. B 43. C 44. B 45. B 46. A 47. B 48. C 49. D 50. C
51. C 52. A 53. A 54. D 55. A 56. A 57. A 58. B 59. E 60. B
61. E 62. B 63. B 64. E 65. A 66. C 67. D 68. E 69. C 70. C
71. D 72. C 73. D 74. B 75. D 76. A 77. D 78. C 79. E 80. D

Part III. Punctuation

	Correct Letter	*Page Number(s)*		*Correct Letter*	*Page Number(s)*
81.	C	281–82	91.	B	294
82.	A	294	92.	E	– – –
83.	A	284	93.	D	300
84.	B	280–81	94.	B	comma not needed
85.	A	293			
86.	B	292–93	95.	A	300
87.	D	300	96.	E	– – –
88.	E	– – –	97.	B	295–96
89.	C	287	98.	D	288
90.	A	291–92	99.	D	285
			100.	A	295